4/08

CONSUMER RIGHTS LAW

Revised and Updated

by

Margaret C. Jasper

2nd Edition

Oceana's Legal Almanac Series:
Law for the Layperson

Oceana®
NEW YORK

OXFORD

UNIVERSITY PRESS

*Oxford University Press, Inc., publishes works that further Oxford University's
objective of excellence in research, scholarship, and education.*

Copyright © 2008 by Oxford University Press, Inc.
Published by Oxford University Press, Inc.
198 Madison Avenue, New York, New York 10016

Oxford is a registered trademark of Oxford University Press
Oceana is a registered trademark of Oxford University Press, Inc.

Library of Congress Cataloging-in-Publication Data

Jasper, Margaret C.
   Consumer rights law / by Margaret C. Jasper. — 2nd ed.
      p. cm. — (Oceana's legal almanac series: law for the layperson)
   Includes bibliographical references.
   ISBN 978-0-19-533956-7 ((clothbound) : alk. paper)
   1. Consumer protection—Law and legislation—United States—Popular works. 2.
Consumer credit—Law and legislation—United States—Popular works. I. Title.
   KF1610.J37 2007
   343.7307'1—dc22

                                                          2007028643

Note to Readers:
This publication is designed to provide accurate and authoritative information in
regard to the subject matter covered. It is based upon sources believed to be accurate and reliable and is intended to be current as of the time it was written. It is sold
with the understanding that the publisher is not engaged in rendering legal,
accounting, or other professional services. If legal advice or other expert assistance
is required, the services of a competent professional person should be sought. Also,
to confirm that the information has not been affected or changed by recent develop-
ments, traditional legal research techniques should be used, including checking
primary sources where appropriate.

*(Based on the Declaration of Principles jointly adopted by a Committee of the
American Bar Association and a Committee of Publishers and Associations.)*

To My Husband Chris

Your love and support

are my motivation and inspiration

To my sons, Michael, Nick and Chris

-and-

In memory of my son, Jimmy

Table of Contents

CHAPTER 4:
CONSUMER BANKING

CHAPTER 5:
AUTOMOBILES

CHAPTER 6:
PRIVACY RIGHTS AND THE INTERNET

ABOUT THE AUTHOR

MARGARET C. JASPER is an attorney engaged in the general practice of law in South Salem, New York, concentrating in the areas of personal injury and entertainment law. Ms. Jasper holds a Juris Doctor degree from Pace University School of Law, White Plains, New York, is a member of the New York and Connecticut bars, and is certified to practice before the United States District Courts for the Southern and Eastern Districts of New York, the United States Court of Appeals for the Second Circuit, and the United States Supreme Court.

Ms. Jasper has been appointed to the law guardian panel for the Family Court of the State of New York, is a member of a number of professional organizations and associations, and is a New York State licensed real estate broker operating as Jasper Real Estate, in South Salem, New York.

Margaret Jasper maintains a website at http://www.JasperLawOffice.com.

In 2004, Ms. Jasper successfully argued a case before the New York Court of Appeals, which gives mothers of babies who are stillborn due to medical negligence the right to bring a legal action and recover emotional distress damages. This successful appeal overturned a 26-year old New York case precedent, which previously prevented mothers of stillborn babies from suing their negligent medical providers.

Ms. Jasper is the author and general editor of the following legal almanacs:

AIDS Law
The Americans with Disabilities Act
Animal Rights Law
Auto Leasing
Bankruptcy Law for the Individual Debtor
Banks and their Customers
Becoming a Citizen

Buying and Selling Your Home
Commercial Law
Consumer Rights and the Law
Co-ops and Condominiums: Your Rights and Obligations As Owner
Copyright Law
Credit Cards and the Law
Custodial Rights
Dealing with Debt
Dictionary of Selected Legal Terms
Drunk Driving Law
DWI, DUI and the Law
Education Law
Elder Law
Employee Rights in the Workplace
Employment Discrimination Under Title VII
Environmental Law
Estate Planning
Everyday Legal Forms
Executors and Personal Representatives: Rights and Responsibilities
Harassment in the Workplace
Health Care and Your Rights
Health Care Directives
Hiring Household Help and Contractors: Your Rights and Obligations Under the Law
Home Mortgage Law Primer
Hospital Liability Law
How To Change Your Name
How To Form an LLC
How To Protect Your Challenged Child
How To Start Your Own Business
Identity Theft and How To Protect Yourself
Individual Bankruptcy and Restructuring
Injured on the Job: Employee Rights, Worker's Compensation and Disability Insurance Law
International Adoption
Juvenile Justice and Children's Law
Labor Law
Landlord-Tenant Law
Law for the Small Business Owner
The Law of Attachment and Garnishment
The Law of Buying and Selling
The Law of Capital Punishment

The Law of Child Custody
The Law of Contracts
The Law of Debt Collection
The Law of Dispute Resolution
The Law of Immigration
The Law of Libel and Slander
The Law of Medical Malpractice
The Law of No-Fault Insurance
The Law of Obscenity and Pornography
The Law of Personal Injury
The Law of Premises Liability
The Law of Product Liability
The Law of Speech and the First Amendment
Lemon Laws
Living Together: Practical Legal Issues
Marriage and Divorce
Missing and Exploited Children: How to Protect Your Child
Motor Vehicle Law
Nursing Home Negligence
Patent Law
Pet Law
Prescription Drugs
Privacy and the Internet: Your Rights and Expectations Under the Law
Probate Law
Protecting Your Business: Disaster Preparation and the Law
Real Estate Law for the Homeowner and Broker
Religion and the Law
Retirement Planning
The Right to Die
Rights of Single Parents
Small Claims Court
Social Security Law
Special Education Law
Teenagers and Substance Abuse
Trademark Law
Trouble Next Door: What to do With Your Neighbor
Victim's Rights Law
Violence Against Women
Welfare: Your Rights and the Law
What if It Happened to You: Violent Crimes and Victims' Rights
What if the Product Doesn't Work: Warranties & Guarantees

Workers' Compensation Law
Your Child's Legal Rights: An Overview
Your Rights in a Class Action Suit
Your Rights as a Tenant
Your Rights Under the Family and Medical Leave Act
You've Been Fired: Your Rights and Remedies

INTRODUCTION

This legal Almanac explores the area of law which governs consumer rights. A consumer is generally defined as an individual who purchases goods and services for his or her personal use. Until the consumer rights movement gained momentum in the mid-1960s, most consumers stood on unequal ground in negotiating transactions with sellers of goods and services. This Almanac gives an overview of the history of the consumer rights movement as it gained momentum over the past several decades.

This Almanac also discusses legislation subsequently passed in an attempt to provide equality in the marketplace and afford the consumer a variety of remedies. Although protective legislation is in effect to benefit the consumer, it is complex. Most consumers are not aware of their rights under the law, and even if they are aware, it takes a certain degree of sophistication to understand exactly what the law provides.

This Almanac provides the consumer with an overview of the law applicable to consumer transactions. The protection and remedies a consumer is entitled to when involved in certain common transactions are explored, as well as advice in handling such transactions. This Almanac further provides the consumer with information concerning the major federal agencies entrusted with overseeing important consumer-related concerns such as product safety. The topics of banking, managing credit, privacy issues and identity protection are explored. The consumer's rights as a patient and a tenant are also examined in this Almanac.

It is important that the individual consumer is made aware of his or her rights, so he or she can recognize a violation when it occurs, and pursue appropriate remedies against the offending party. An informed consumer benefits not only the individual, but the society of consumers as they work to gain equality in the marketplace.

The Appendix provides directories of agencies concerned with consumer rights, including the major federal agencies entrusted with overseeing important consumer-related concerns such as product safety and environmental and occupational safety. The Appendix also sets forth the text of applicable statutes, and other pertinent information and data. The Glossary contains definitions of many of the terms used throughout the Almanac.

CHAPTER 1:
AN OVERVIEW OF CONSUMER
RIGHTS LAW

HISTORY OF THE CONSUMER PROTECTION MOVEMENT

Prior to World War I, there was little legislation in place to protect the consumer against unfair treatment in the marketplace. Society was not ready to impose its own set of criteria on what was perceived to be an individual's personal problem. This was largely due to the fact that most consumer transactions were conducted in small communities, on a personal level, with a local vendor. A certain degree of fairness and ethical behavior was expected when dealing on such a small-scale basis.

As the industrial revolution took hold, and business which was once conducted on a personal level gave way to mass production and consumption, the fairness and equality amongst individuals in the marketplace gave way to a new system. And, while the merchants became more sophisticated, the consumer was relegated to an inferior position at the bargaining table.

For those who, by reason of their wealth, had access to the courts, there were remedies in tort and contract available when the need arose. However, the majority of consumers did not have such access. "Caveat emptor"—a Latin phrase meaning "buyer beware"—adequately summed up the unsophisticated consumer's standing when dealing with the sellers of goods and services.

Unfortunately, whereas that concept may have once had some validity when both consumer and seller were more equally matched, it now subjected the consumer to exploitation. This inequality spawned a consumer rights movement in the mid-1960s and 1970s that fought for legislation to supplement the general common law remedies with statutes that governed consumer transactions. Presently, there are numerous private and government organizations that assist consumers with all types of transactions and services, many of which specialize in particular areas.

CONSUMER ASSISTANCE ORGANIZATIONS

There are a number of private and government organizations at the local, state and federal level which are designed to assist the consumer, and protect and advocate for the consumer's rights.

The Federal Citizen Information Center

The Federal Citizen Information Center (FCIC), a department of the U.S. General Services Administration, publishes the Consumer Action Handbook that provides helpful information and resource directories for consumers. Free copies of the 2007 Consumer Action Handbook are available by contacting the FCIC, as follows:

Online Request

You can request a copy of the Consumer Action Handbook by visiting the FCIC website: www.consumeraction.gov.

Written Request

You can request a copy of the Consumer Action Handbook by writing to the FCIC as follows:

The Federal Citizen Information Center

U.S. General Services Administration

1800 F Street NW, Room G142

Washington, DC 20405

Tel: 202-501-1794

Website: www.consumeraction.gov

National Consumer Organizations

For assistance at the national level, there are many national organizations whose missions are defined as consumer assistance, protection and/or advocacy. Among other things, these organizations assist consumers with their problems and concerns, and develop educational materials for consumers.

A directory of National Consumer Organizations is set forth in Appendix 1.

State Consumer Protection Offices

State and local consumer protection offices work to resolve consumer complaints and distribute consumer education information. Some offices investigate and prosecute offenders, as well as mediate disputes.

A directory of state Consumer Protection Agencies is set forth in Appendix 2.

The Better Business Bureau

If you are buying goods or services from a business that is new or not yet well-established, you can check the company out with your local Better Business Bureau (BBB) to see whether any complaints have been filed against the company. The BBB is a non-profit organization supported primarily by local businesses. The focus of the BBB is to promote an ethical marketplace by encouraging honest advertising and selling practices.

The BBB offers the consumer a variety of services, including:

1. General information on products or services;

2. Business reliability reports;

3. Background information on businesses, organizations and charities;

4. Consumer education programs; and

5. Arbitration and mediation services.

The Council of Better Business Bureaus (CBBB) is the umbrella organization for the BBB branches, and is supported by national companies and the BBB branches. There are local branches of the BBB across the United States. You can find your local BBB branch by contacting CBBB headquarters, as follows:

The Council of Better Business Bureaus

4200 Wilson Boulevard, Suite 800

Arlington, VA 22203-1838

Telephone: 1-703-276-0100

Fax: 1-703-525-8277

Website: www.bbb.org

Corporate Consumer Relations Departments

Many companies have organized in-house consumer relations departments to address consumer concerns and help resolve consumer complaints. You can find out whether a certain company has a consumer relations department by contacting that company's headquarters.

Automobile Manufacturers

Most automobile manufacturers have organized national or regional offices to handle consumer complaints which are not resolved by the local car dealer. You can find out whether a certain automobile manufacturer has a consumer relations department by contacting that company's headquarters.

Consumer rights in automobile purchases and leases are discussed more fully in Chapter 5, Automobiles.

Trade Associations

Many trade associations, such as those which govern the insurance and banking industries, have established programs to help consumers resolve complaints.

Consumer rights in banking and finance are discussed more fully in Chapter 4, Consumer Banking.

Professional Associations

Nearly all professional associations, such as those which govern doctors, lawyers and accountants, have established offices that investigate complaints and grievances filed by the public and/or can provide you with information and resources, as follows:

The American Medical Association (AMA)

515 N. State Street
Chicago, IL 60610
(800) 621-8335
Website: www.ama-assn.org

The American Bar Association (ABA)

321 N. Clark Street
Chicago, IL 60610
(800) 285-2221
Website: www.abanet.org

The American Institute of Certified Public Accountants (AICPA)

1211 Avenue of the Americas
New York, NY 10036
Telephone: (212) 596-6200
Website: www.aicpa

Consumer Credit Counseling Services

Consumer Credit Counseling services provide the consumer with assistance in budgeting money and handling debt. These services are usually sponsored by credit unions, family service centers, and religious organizations, and offer some type of free or low-cost credit counseling.

Consumer credit and debt is discussed more fully in Chapter 3, The Consumer Credit Protection Act.

Consumer Advocacy Groups

There are a number of private and voluntary consumer organizations that advocate specific consumer interests. They assist consumers with their concerns and help file complaints, however, they have no enforcement authority. To find a consumer advocacy group located near you, contact your state consumer protection agency, as set forth in Appendix 2, (Directory of State Consumer Protection Agencies).

The consumer rights groups that sprung up in the late 20th century were able to push through federal and state legislation which finally addressed the consumer's concerns for equality in the marketplace. As set forth below, a number of statutes were passed which provide the consumer a variety of remedies. Many statutes also provide an award for reasonable legal fees to successful litigants, thus opening the courts to those who are financially unable to seek justice.

THE FEDERAL TRADE COMMISSION ACT

The Federal Trade Commission ("FTC") was originally established in 1914 to enforce antitrust legislation. Under the Federal Trade Commission Act, unfair methods of competition among businesses were thus prohibited. This early legislation did not involve practices that directly involved the individual consumer.

The FTC Act – Unfair or Deceptive Acts or Practices

The FTC subsequently found that unfair or deceptive acts or practices in the marketplace were also negatively impacting honest competition. Therefore, the FTC determined that this unfair method of competition fell under FTC jurisdiction. Once this determination was made, the FTC claimed its authority over consumer-related matters, and the Federal Trade Commission Act was subsequently amended to give the FTC broader authority over consumer rights.

State Statutes Governing Unfair or Deceptive Acts or Practices

Following the federal example, state legislatures thereafter began passing their own consumer protection statutes, which are often referred to as "Little FTCs." All jurisdictions now have some sort of legislation aimed at protecting consumers from unfair or deceptive acts or practices by sellers of goods and services in the marketplace.

Noncompliance with such a statute is generally known as a "UDAP" violation. Most state statutes have utilized the language set forth in Section 5(a)(1) of the Federal Trade Commission Act that prohibits unfair or deceptive acts or practices and unfair methods of competition. These state statutes have various names according to the jurisdiction, such as consumer protection statutes, unfair trade statutes, etc.

A table of state statutes governing unfair or deceptive acts or practices is set forth in Appendix 3.

An aggrieved consumer can bring a lawsuit alleging a UDAP violation. In order to prevail, the consumer must be able to demonstrate that a particular act or practice is unfair or deceptive. Before making a decision to proceed, one must determine whether the act or practice is prohibited by the consumer protection statute of the applicable jurisdiction. A careful examination of the statute is crucial because the consumer generally has the burden of proving that the statute applies.

Presently, the general standard of proof requires nothing more than a showing that the practice has a tendency or capacity to deceive a significant minority of consumers by a preponderance of the evidence.

Some state consumer protection statutes provide that certain conditions must be met before the consumer is permitted to file an action, such as a mandatory settlement conference. In addition, some states require the consumer to have actually suffered damages before bringing an action. However, the amount of damages suffered is generally irrelevant, and even minimal damages usually satisfy the statute.

Some states require the consumer to send the seller a notice or demand letter before filing a lawsuit. The purpose for this requirement is to give the seller an opportunity to settle the matter so as to avoid flooding the courts with numerous consumer actions.

In addition, one must determine the statute of limitations period within which the claim must be initiated. In general, the statute begins to run from the time a reasonable person would have discovered the facts constituting the unfair or deceptive act or practice. In most cases, a lawsuit cannot be commenced once the statutory period has expired. The reader is advised to check the law of his or her own jurisdiction to determine the applicable statute of limitations.

The Per Se Violation

A per se violation is deemed to occur when a practice clearly violates a specific statutory guideline. Most state consumer protection statutes set forth enumerated statutory violations as well as a catchall provision for all other unfair or deceptive acts or practices.

It is preferable for the consumer to demonstrate to the court that the act is a per se violation rather than leave it up to the court to determine whether it falls within the catchall provision. If a per se violation is demonstrated, the court need only consider whether the act falls within the specific guidelines of the consumer protection statute.

The Non Per Se Violation

If a particular act or practice does not violate one of the enumerated prohibitions of a state's consumer protection statute, it may nonetheless be a violation. In such a case, the consumer must demonstrate liability to the court. This may be accomplished by setting forth a detailed account of the unfair and/or deceptive act or practice, stating favorable case law concerning similar complaints, and showing how the practice violates the general standards of deception or unfairness.

Further, because most state consumer protection statutes are modeled after the Federal Trade Commission Act, one may look to the Act, and cases decided under the Act, for guidance in determining whether a particular act or practice is prohibited.

Damages

The reason a consumer brings an action under the state consumer protection statute is to find a remedy for the damages that he or she suffered as a result of the seller's unfair or deceptive act or practice. If the statute did not provide a remedy, there would be little reason to spend one's time, energy and financial resources in bringing the claim.

A common remedy sought is a court-ordered injunction to prevent the seller from engaging in the prohibited conduct. The purpose of the injunction is to put the seller on notice that certain practices are prohibited, and to order the seller not to continue the prohibited practice. Other remedies include voiding or rescinding a contract, and an award of monetary damages.

A consumer who prevails may be entitled to actual damages, such as out-of-pocket expenses. Restitution is another available remedy. Damages for pain and suffering may also be awarded. However, if the consumer's claim alleges mental anguish, there may be certain additional prerequisites to recovery—e.g., physical manifestation of the mental anguish—depending on the jurisdiction.

Because attorney fees may be cost prohibitive in bringing a small consumer claim, some states have also begun to award attorneys fees in addition to any monetary damage award to the consumer.

It is the consumer's responsibility to prove that he or she suffered damages, and to demonstrate how those damages are related to the

UDAP violation. Some statutes provide for minimum damage awards to plaintiffs who are able to prove that a violation has occurred. Multiple damage awards, e.g. treble damages, are available in some states provided actual damages are proven. Further, where the seller's malice or reckless conduct is proven, punitive damages may be available in some jurisdictions.

Class Actions

An effective method of deterring unfair or deceptive acts or practices by a particular seller is to join a number of small consumer claims into a class action. Procedures for bringing a consumer class action would be governed by the jurisdiction's class action statute unless the applicable consumer protection statute sets forth its own class action provisions.

Make an Informed Purchase

When making a purchase, particularly a large purchase, don't be afraid to ask all of the questions you need to, in order to feel comfortable about the purchase. It is your money and you can spend it wherever you choose. Don't let high pressure sales tactics force you into making a hasty decision. It is preferable that you leave the establishment and take some time to carefully consider the purchase.

Bait and Switch

Many businesses lure buyers into their store by advertising items on "sale." A common selling tactic, known as "bait and switch," occurs when the consumer inquires about the sale item but is instead steered towards a higher priced item. Don't let yourself be a victim of this tactic. If you are told that the sale item is not available, or are otherwise deterred from inquiring about the sale item, leave the establishment and take your business elsewhere.

Sales and Lowest Price Guarantees

Further, while you should try and take advantage of sale items, take the time to compare prices with other sellers to make sure you are really getting a bargain. Remember, all the merchandise in the store is offered for "sale." That doesn't mean you are getting a break on the price. An item that may be on "sale" in one store can more than likely be found in another store at the same or lower price.

Also, make sure that there are no "hidden" charges associated with your purchase that are not included in the total cost. Some merchants may try to compensate for their "sales" by assessing delivery charges, installation fees, etc.

In addition, some stores will guarantee their price as the lowest available price for that item. They claim that they will refund the difference if the consumer subsequently finds the same item on sale at another store for a lesser price. However, in order to take advantage of this guarantee, the consumer usually has to provide the seller with some proof that the item was actually on sale for a lesser price during the same time period, to qualify for the refund, e.g. an advertisement, etc.

Refunds and Exchange Policies

Prior to making your purchase, you should ask about the merchant's refund or exchange policy and have it reduced to writing as part of the transaction. Read the warranty provisions to ascertain your rights should you encounter a problem with the product.

After you have made the purchase, keep a file containing the sales receipt, warranty card, service contract and instructions. Familiarize yourself with the service and warranty provisions for the product, and how your use of the product may affect those rights. If you encounter problems with the item, contact the company for instructions. Keep a journal of your telephone calls, including the name and title of the representative who handles your call. If you are unable to resolve your problem at the local level, contact the company's headquarters, in writing.

Whenever you mail correspondence, send it certified mail with a return receipt requested so you can establish the date your complaint was made. Always send photocopies only of any supporting documentation, such as your sales receipt or warranty. Keep your originals in a safe place.

If the problem is still not resolved to your satisfaction, contact your local or state consumer protection agency to make a complaint, and seek further advice in pursuing your claim.

Plain Language Statutes

Most people have been confronted with a contract or agreement that contains numerous paragraphs of fine print written in "legalese." Such language is common in standard form contracts, such as leases, purchase agreements, and consumer credit agreements. This creates a dilemma for the layperson because such transactions are not commonly those for which spending legal fees are anticipated or desirable. Therefore, most people make an attempt at deciphering the contract language without legal guidance, and end up signing an agreement without a complete understanding of its terms.

Largely due to the consumer activist movement, various state legislatures have attempted to address this problem by enacting "Plain Language" laws which require that certain consumer contracts be written so that the average layperson can understand them.

The two general categories of plain language laws which have been enacted are the (1) general/subjective plain language laws; and the (2) specific/objective plain language laws.

The general/subjective plain language laws require the drafter to ensure the language contained in the contract is sufficiently clear, containing common usage words, so that the layperson can understand what they are signing. In addition, the layout of the contract is generally required to be clearly set forth, with its various sections appropriately labeled and subdivided.

The specific/objective plain language laws set forth an elaborate scoring system which must be adhered to in order to be deemed acceptable. A common objective test used in specific/subjective plain language statutes is known as the Flesch test of reading ease. The Flesch test computes a score based on the measurement of the number of syllables in each word and the number of words in each sentence.

The theory behind this objective test is that shorter words in shorter sentences are more easily understood. In addition to the Flesch test, there are certain specific requirements concerning the size of the type and layout of the contract.

If you are required to sign a purchase agreement as part of a lease or purchase, make sure all of the blank spaces are filled in and read the agreement carefully before signing. If you don't understand the terms, don't sign it. Don't rely on the explanation of the merchant. If your understanding is not in writing, it will be your word against the salesperson and you may not have any legal recourse to enforce an oral promise.

The Federal Trade Commission Cooling Off Rule – Your Cancellation Rights

Door-to-door sales are no longer as popular as in previous decades, particularly if the consumer is not given advance notice to set up an appointment. This may be attributed to the growing crime problem, and the reluctance of individuals to open their home to strangers. There have been many reported incidents concerning criminals using fake identification and uniforms to gain access to a person's home to commit a crime.

Thus, if you are confronted with a door-to-door salesperson, you should ask to see his or her personal photo identification. Before letting the salesperson in your home, call the company and confirm that the person is a legitimate employee.

Also, be aware that the cost of products sold in this manner are usually considerably higher than purchasing the product at a store. If you feel that you are being pressured into making a purchase, ask the salesperson to leave the literature and advise him or her that you have to take time to consider the purchase.

If you do decide to make a purchase from a door-to-door salesperson, under the law, you are entitled to cancel the sale if the cost of the item is $25 or more. The Federal Trade Commission (FTC) Cooling-Off Rule applies to sales at the buyer's home, workplace or dormitory, or at a facility rented by the seller on a temporary or short-term basis, such as a hotel or motel room, convention center, etc. The law applies even when you invite the salesperson to make a presentation in your home.

Under the law, the salesperson is required to tell you about your cancellation rights at the time of the sale. The salesperson must also give you two copies of a cancellation form and a copy of your contract or receipt. The contract or receipt should be dated, show the name and address of the seller, and explain your right to cancel. You don't need to give a reason for canceling the sale. You can simply change your mind.

If you decide to cancel the purchase, you must notify the company, in writing, by midnight of the third business day following the sale, excluding Sunday and holidays. The cancellation notice should be mailed by certified mail with a return receipt requested to establish the date it was mailed. You are entitled to a refund within 10 days. The seller must retrieve the item within 20 days or in the alternative, the seller must reimburse you for shipping expenses, if you elect to ship the package.

The Federal Trade Commission (FTC) Telemarketing Sales Rule

In August 1994, the Telemarketing and Consumer Fraud and Abuse Prevention Act became law. The purpose of the Act is to aid law enforcement agencies in their fight against telemarketing fraud, and to give consumers new protections and guidance on how to tell the difference between fraudulent and legitimate telemarketing.

Under the Act, the FTC implemented the Telemarketing Sales Rule to achieve those goals. The key provisions of the Rule require specific disclosures, prohibit misrepresentations, set limits on the times telemarketers may call consumers, prohibit calls after a consumer asks not to be called, set payment restrictions for the sale of certain goods and services, and require that specific business records be kept for two years.

The Telemarketing Sales Rule covers telemarketing—i.e., any plan, program, or campaign to sell goods or services through interstate telephone calls. Exceptions exist for: (1) certain financial institutions, such as banks and credit unions; (2) common carriers, such as long-distance telephone companies and airlines; (3) non-profit organizations; and (4) insurance companies.

Required Disclosure

The Rule requires a seller or telemarketer, whether making outbound calls to consumers or receiving inbound calls from consumers, to provide certain material information before that consumer pays for goods or services that are the subject of the sales offer. Material information is information that would likely affect a person's choice of goods or services, or their conduct regarding them—i.e, information necessary for a consumer to make an informed purchasing decision.

Misrepresentation

The Rule generally prohibits a seller or telemarketer from making any false or misleading statement to induce anyone to pay for goods or services. For example, telemarketers cannot falsely claim that they need to obtain a consumer's bank account number or credit card number only for identification purposes, when in fact they use those numbers to obtain payment for the goods or services offered.

Calling Restrictions

In addition, the Rule imposes calling restrictions and prohibits telemarketers from:

1. Calling consumers repeatedly or continuously, with the intent to annoy, abuse, or harass any person at the called number;

2. Calling any consumer who previously has requested that he or she not be called again—the "do not call" provision as further discussed below; or

3. Calling any consumer's residence before 8:00 A.M. or after 9:00 PM. local time at the consumer's location.

The "Do Not Call" Provision

Under the Act, a telemarketer may not call a consumer who previously has requested to receive no more calls from, or on behalf of, a particular seller whose goods or services are being offered. Similarly, a seller that has been requested by a consumer not to call again may not cause a telemarketer to call that consumer.

Sellers and telemarketers are responsible for keeping "do not call lists" of those consumers who have requested not to receive calls placed by, or on behalf of, a particular seller. Calling a consumer who has requested not to be called is a Rule violation and a telemarketer or seller that engages in the practice of making such calls risks a $10,000 civil penalty per violation.

If a consumer is called who has requested not to be called by or on behalf of a particular seller, the seller and telemarketer may be liable for a Rule violation. If an enforcement investigation finds that neither the seller nor the telemarketer had written "do not call" procedures in place, both would be liable for the Rule violation.

If the investigation reveals that the seller had written "do not call" procedures but the telemarketer ignored the procedures, the telemarketer would be liable for the Rule violation. The seller may also be liable if the investigation finds that the seller did not implement its written procedures. Ultimately a seller is responsible for keeping a current "do not call" list, whether it is through a telemarketing service it hires or through its own efforts.

If a seller or telemarketer has and implements written "do not call" procedures, it will not be liable for a Rule violation if a subsequent call is the result of error, but it may be subject to an enforcement investigation. The investigation would focus on the effectiveness of the procedures in place, how they are implemented, and if all personnel are trained in the "do not call" procedures. If there is a high incidence of "errors," it may be determined that the procedures are inadequate to comply with the Rule's "do not call" requirements and thus there is a Rule violation. On the other hand, if there is a low incidence of "errors," there may not be a Rule violation.

The FTC Do Not Call Registry

Many businesses, including legitimate businesses, use the telephone to market their goods and services. Nevertheless, the consumer must be careful when dealing with any person over the telephone. For example, unless you are familiar with the particular company, you should refrain from giving personal information over the telephone, such as credit card numbers, checking account numbers, etc. To protect consumers from unscrupulous telemarketers, and make it easier and more efficient for consumers to stop receiving unwanted telemarketing calls, the Federal government created the national "Do Not Call Registry," a free service administered by the Federal Trade Commission (FTC).

You can stop telemarketing calls by registering your home telephone number or cell phone number—business and fax numbers are not covered—with the FTC Do Not Call Registry, as follows:

Online Registration

Register online at the FTC website: www.donotcall.gov/.

Telephone Registration

> Register by telephone at the FTC toll-free number: 1-888-382-1222. You must place the call from the number you wish to register.

Most telemarketers will not call your number once it has been on the registry for 31 days. If they do, you can file a complaint at the FTC registry website. Your registration will be effective for five years.

Enforcement and Penalties

The Federal Trade Commission, the states, and private persons may bring civil law enforcement actions in federal district courts to enforce the Rule. Actions by the states may be brought by either the attorney general of the state or by any other state officer authorized by the state to bring actions on behalf of its residents. Private persons may bring an action to enforce the Rule if they have suffered $50,000 or more in actual damages. Anyone who violates the Rule is subject to civil penalties of up to $10,000 per violation. In addition, violators may be subject to nation-wide injunctions that prohibit certain conduct, and may be required to pay redress to injured consumers.

The Federal Trade Commission Mail or Telephone Order Merchandise Rule

Mail and telephone order businesses are governed by federal law. The Federal Trade Commission (FTC) Mail or Telephone Order Merchandise Rule—also referred to as the 30-day Rule—applies to most goods a consumer orders from the business by mail, telephone, fax, or on the Internet. It does not matter how the merchandise is advertised, how the customer pays, or who initiates the contact.

Under the law, when a business advertises merchandise, it must follow certain rules concerning shipment of the merchandise, as follows:

1. The company is required to ship the consumer's mail order merchandise within 30 days of receiving the order unless otherwise stated in the advertisement.

2. The company is required to notify the consumer if the shipment cannot be made on time, and to give the consumer the right to either cancel the shipment and receive a refund, or agree to a revised shipping date.

3. If the consumer cancels an order that was not timely shipped, he or she has the right to a refund within 7 days. If the item was charged, a credit should issue within one billing cycle.

In order to take advantage of the federal protection afforded the consumer, an accurate record of all mail order purchases should be maintained, including:

1. The company name, address and phone number;

2. The date of order;

3. An item description;

4. The amount of purchase;

5. The method of purchase (e.g. check or credit card, etc.); and

6. The promised delivery date.

State law may afford the consumer further protection for mail and telephone order purchases, thus, the reader is advised to check the law of his or her own jurisdiction.

Selected provisions of the FTC Mail or Telephone Order Merchandise Rule is set forth in Appendix 4.

THE FTC FUNERAL RULE

When a family member passes away, the surviving loved ones are faced with a lot of difficult and emotional decisions to make in a very short period of time. Planning a funeral ranks among one of the most expensive purchases a consumer will ever make, ranging from $6,000 to $10,000 and upward.

Unfortunately, many unscrupulous funeral providers take advantage of the situation and try to push special "package deals" of goods and services at a time when family members are most vulnerable. They inflate prices, overcharge, or try to get grieving family members to purchase expensive products and unnecessary services.

Recognizing the problem, the federal government enacted the "Funeral Rule" to advise consumers of their rights during this difficult time. The Funeral Rule is enforced by the Federal Trade Commission (FTC).

Consumer's Rights

Under the Funeral Rule:

1. The consumer has the right to choose the individual funeral goods and services he or she wants and/or needs, with some limited exceptions.

2. The funeral provider must state this right in writing on the general price list.

3. If state or local law requires the consumer to buy any particular item, the funeral provider must disclose it on the price list, with a reference to the specific law.

4. The funeral provider may not refuse, or charge a fee, to handle a casket the consumer bought elsewhere.

5. The funeral provider that offers cremations must make alternative containers available—i.e., you are not required to purchase a casket for cremation.

Under the funeral rule, you do not have to purchase a "package" deal. You have the right to purchase the individual goods and services you want and/or need. If you want to buy a casket, the funeral provider must show you descriptions of the available selections and the prices before actually showing you the caskets. State laws regarding funerals and burials vary, therefore, the reader is advised to check the law of his or her jurisdiction concerning the types of goods or services the law requires a consumer to purchase, and which ones are optional.

After you have settled on the goods and services you want and need, but before you pay, you are entitled to receive a written statement showing exactly what you are buying and the cost of each item. Immediately after making the arrangements, the funeral home must give you a statement listing every good and service you have selected, the price of each, and the total cost immediately after you make the arrangements.

Prepaid Funeral Arrangements

Many consumers enter into contracts to prearrange their funeral and prepay some or all of the related expenses. State laws govern the prepayment of funeral goods and services. Various states have laws to help ensure that these advance payments are available to pay for the funeral products and services when they are needed. But protections vary widely from state to state, and some state laws offer little or no effective protection. Some state laws require the funeral home or cemetery to place a percentage of the prepayment in a state-regulated trust or to purchase a life insurance policy with the death benefits assigned to the funeral home or cemetery.

According to the FTC, if you are considering pre-paying for funeral goods and services, the following should be considered:

1. What are you are paying for? Are you buying only merchandise, like a casket and vault, or are you purchasing funeral services as well?

2. What happens to the money you have prepaid? States have different requirements for handling funds paid for prearranged funeral services.

3. What happens to the interest income on money that is prepaid and put into a trust account?

4. Are you protected if the firm you dealt with goes out of business?

5. Can you cancel the contract and get a full refund if you change your mind?

6. What happens if you move to a different area or die while away from home? Some prepaid funeral plans can be transferred, but often at an added cost.

CHAPTER 2:
CONSUMER PRODUCT SAFETY

FEDERAL REGULATION OF CONSUMER PRODUCT SAFETY

A number of federal agencies have jurisdiction over the safety of certain categories of consumer products. The major federal agencies, their jurisdiction, role and purpose are set forth below.

The U.S. Consumer Product Safety Commission

The U.S. Consumer Product Safety Commission (CPSC) is an independent federal regulatory agency created by Congress in 1972 under the Consumer Product Safety Act. The CPSC's mission is to protect the public from unreasonable risks of serious injury or death from more than 15,000 types of consumer products under the agency's jurisdiction.

Deaths, injuries and property damage from consumer product incidents cost the nation more than $700 billion annually. The CPSC is committed to protecting consumers and families from products that pose a fire, electrical, chemical, or mechanical hazard, and products that can injure children. The CPSC is largely responsible for a 30 % decline in the rate of deaths and injuries associated with consumer products over the past 30 years.

The CPSC operates a hotline which provides the consumer with information on product recalls and the safe use of the products it regulates. The hotline staff also accepts and investigates consumer reports of unsafe products. The hotline staff may be reached from 8:30 am – 5:00 pm ET. Messages may be left at any time.

Contact information for CPSC Headquarters is as follows:

The U.S. Consumer Product Safety Commission
4330 East West Highway
Bethesda, MD 20814

Telephone: 301-504-7923
Fax: 301-504-0124
E-mail: info@cpsc.gov
Website: www.cpsc.gov
Toll-Free Consumer Hotline: 1-800-638-2772 (24 hours/7 days)

A directory of U.S. Consumer Product Safety Commission Regional Offices is set forth in Appendix 5.

The National Highway Traffic Safety Administration

The National Highway Traffic Safety Administration ("NHTSA") was established by the Highway Safety Act of 1970 under the jurisdiction of the U.S. Department of Transportation. The NHTSA is responsible for reducing fatalities, injuries and economic losses resulting from motor vehicle accidents.

The NHTSA accomplishes its goals by researching, promulgating and enforcing safety performance standards for motor vehicles, investigating safety defects in motor vehicles, and sponsoring state and local highway safety programs. The NHTSA also provides consumers with important safety information concerning recalls; standards for child safety seats and seat belts; and consumer fraud issues, such as odometer fraud.

The NHTSA operates a vehicle safety hotline for consumers to report suspected safety defects in their vehicle, vehicle equipment, and child safety seats, and to obtain information about air bags, highway safety, and the proper use of child safety seats.

Contact information for the NHTSA Headquarters is as follows:

The National Highway Traffic Safety Administration

1200 New Jersey Avenue SE

West Building

Washington, DC 20590

Telephone: 1-888-327-4236

Website: www.nhtsa.gov

A directory of National Highway Traffic Safety Administration Regional Offices is set forth in Appendix 6.

The U.S. Food and Drug Administration

The U.S. Food and Drug Administration ("FDA") is one of the nation's oldest consumer protection agencies. It is a public health agency responsible for protecting consumers through the enforcement of the Federal Food, Drug and Cosmetic Act, as well as related public health laws. The FDA operates under the jurisdiction of the U.S. Department of Health and Human Services.

The FDA governs the following products:

1. Food (excluding meat and poultry which is regulated by the U.S. Department of Agriculture);

2. Cosmetics;

3. Drugs, including prescription drugs and over-the-counter medications;

4. Medical devices, e.g., pacemakers, hearing aids, and contact lenses, etc.;

5. Biological products, e.g., vaccinations and blood products, etc.;

6. Animal food and drugs for pets and farm animals;

7. Radiation emitting products, e.g., cell phones, lasers, and microwave ovens, etc.; and

8. Combination products, i.e., a product made up of two or more FDA-regulated products.

The FDA is responsible for making sure that the products under its jurisdiction are safe and that they include accurate labeling information for their proper use. For example, food manufacturers are required to use a label format that includes complete, useful and accurate nutrition information that must set forth mandatory dietary components of their products.

The FDA receives and investigates consumer complaints about the products under its jurisdiction. If you suspect that a product caused you illness or injury, first determine whether:

1. You used the product for its intended purpose;

2. You carefully followed the instructions for the product;

3. You used the product prior to its labeled expiration date; and

4. You did not have any medical condition that would have caused the illness or injury.

If you ruled out all of the above as possible reasons for experiencing a problem with an FDA-regulated product, you should file a report with the FDA as soon as possible after encountering the problem. Keep the remainder of the product, if any, for testing purposes.

Contact information for the FDA Headquarters is as follows:

The U.S. Food and Drug Administration
5600 Fishers Lane

Rockville, Maryland 20857
Washington, DC 20590
Telephone: 1-888-463-6332
Website: www.fda.gov

A directory of U.S. Food and Drug Administration Regional Offices is set forth in Appendix 7.

The U.S. Environmental Protection Agency

The U.S. Environmental Protection Agency (EPA) was created in 1970 in response to the growing public demand for cleaner water, air and land. Prior to the establishment of the EPA, the federal government did not have an agency responsible for a coordinated implementation of the federal laws designed to protect the environment.

The primary mission of the U.S. Environmental Protection Agency ("EPA") is to protect human health and to safeguard and improve the natural environment—air, water and land—upon which human life depends. The EPA implements programs under numerous environmental statutes including the Clean Water Act, the Clean Air Act, the Safe Drinking Water Act, and the Toxic Substances Control Act, etc.

The EPA's national efforts to reduce environmental risk are based on the best available scientific information. The EPA ensures that all members of society—businesses, state and local governments, communities and citizens—have access to information so that they can become full participants in preventing pollution and protecting human health and the environment.

Concerned consumers can report suspected violations of environmental regulations by contacting their EPA regional office.

Contact information for EPA Headquarters is as follows:

The U.S. Environmental Protection Agency
1200 Pennsylvania Avenue N.W.
Washington, DC 20460
Telephone: 1-202-564-4700
Website: www.epa.gov

A directory of U.S. Environmental Protection Agency Regional Offices is set forth in Appendix 8.

CONSUMER PRODUCT SAFETY LITIGATION

In addition to the protection provided consumers by the above federal agencies, a body of law, generally known as product liability law, has emerged to ensure that unsafe products do not find their way into the hands of the consumer. Product liability law involves the placement of a defective product into the stream of commerce by sellers of the product.

A product is deemed defective if it is unsatisfactory in some way when it reaches the consumer. Responsibility for the defect rests with all sellers of the product who are in the distribution chain. In order to hold the seller of a defective product responsible, it is required that a "sale" takes place. A sale is defined as the passing of title from the seller to the buyer for a price.

The person who is injured by a defective product does not have to be the purchaser of the product in order to be compensated, except in a minority of jurisdictions which require privity of contract to maintain a lawsuit for breach of warranty. The general rule merely requires that it is foreseeable that the plaintiff could have been injured as a result of the defect, in order to recover damages.

The Defective Condition

In order for the consumer to prevail in a product liability lawsuit, he or she must demonstrate that the product was supplied in a defective condition. A defect generally refers to some problem, weakness, omission or error existing in the product that renders it unsafe or unreasonably dangerous. Defects generally fall into three categories: (a) manufacturing defects; (b) design defects; and (c) warning defects.

Manufacturing Defects

A manufacturing defect exists when the product does not conform to the manufacturer's own specifications. The defect generally occurs randomly. Unlike other types of defects, when a manufacturing defect is found to be the cause of a consumer's injury, the doctrine of strict liability is imposed—i.e., the consumer doesn't have to prove negligence or fault to prevail in the lawsuit. This is so because fault is assumed when a product's manufacture so blatantly falls below ordinary consumer expectations.

Design Defects

Unlike a manufacturing defect, a design defect refers to a defect common to the product itself, and not occurring in a random sample. Thus, the defect is usually applicable to the whole line of products. For example, a product may be designed defectively if it is found that it fails to perform safely according to ordinary consumer expectations. Further, a product may be defectively designed if there was a cost-effective alternative design that would have prevented the risk of injury to the consumer.

Although a design defect claim often requires a finding of negligence, strict liability may be imposed for an unreasonably dangerous design if the consumer is able to present evidence that there was a safer design available which was feasible to implement. Further, a product may be deemed unreasonably dangerous even though no safer design was available, in effect determining that the product should never have been manufactured in the first place.

Warning Defects

Warning defects usually involve some written communication accompanying the product. For example, a product may fail to include a warning necessary to the consumer's proper use of the product, rendering it unsafe. This omission may be deemed a warning defect that, in effect, makes the product unreasonably dangerous. Warning defects are often grouped together with design defects because warning defects share some of the same characteristics. For example, a warning defect, like a design defect, typically applies to a whole line of products rather than a random sample.

Misrepresentation

Misrepresentation of a product's capabilities—whether negligent or intentional—may render the seller of a product liable even if the product has no defect. Because the representation itself forms the basis of the consumer's expectation, the standard of implied ordinary consumer expectations is irrelevant. Thus, the "defect" is the misrepresentation.

Criteria to Determine Defectiveness

A variety of tests have been used by the courts to establish whether a product is defective. The most common tests for defectiveness are set forth below.

Ordinary Consumer Expectation

The most common standard by which a product is deemed sold in a defective condition is when it is "dangerous to an extent beyond that which would be contemplated by the ordinary consumer who purchases it, with the ordinary knowledge common to the community as to its characteristics." [Restatement of Torts 2d, Section 402].

Expert Testimony

The ordinary consumer expectation test for defectiveness does not work in all instances. The extent of a defect may not be within the realm of a layperson's knowledge, and expert testimony is then required to demonstrate the presence of a defect.

Risk/Utility Analysis

Courts have also used other tests to determine the defectiveness of a product, including the risk/utility analysis. Under this test, an examination of the cost of making a particular product safer is weighed against the risk of injury present if safety measures are not implemented.

If it is deemed that the cost of safety is less than the risk of injury, then the benefit of changing the product to make it safer outweighs the cost, and the unchanged product is deemed defective. On the other hand, if it is determined that the risk is minimal compared to the cost of changing the product, then the unchanged product would not be deemed defective.

There are seven factors which are commonly considered by courts in this risk/utility analysis:

1. The usefulness and desirability of the product;

2. The likelihood and probable seriousness of injury from the product;

3. The availability of a substitute product that would meet the same need and not be as unsafe;

4. The manufacturer's ability to eliminate the danger without impairing usefulness or making the product too expensive;

5. The user's ability to avoid the danger;

6. The user's anticipated awareness of the danger; and

7. The feasibility on the part of the manufacturer of spreading the risk of loss by pricing or insurance.

The Unavoidably Unsafe Product

The unavoidably unsafe product is one which simply cannot be made safer given present knowledge or technology. Nevertheless, its usefulness outweighs its risks. This scenario is most often found in the area of drugs. However, it is incumbent upon the seller of such products to give proper warnings of the dangers and risks associated with the use of such a product so that the consumer can make an informed decision.

Responsible Parties

Potential liability in a product liability action rests with all of the parties in the chain of distribution and marketing of the product. This generally includes the manufacturer—including the manufacturer of any defective component part—and the seller of the product. When investigating a product liability claim, it is important to identify all potentially responsible parties and gather all other information relevant to the case.

Also included in a product liability action, if applicable to the facts, would be the assembler or installer, and the reseller in the case of a used or reconditioned product. Unless limited by state statute, others may be held liable if it is found that they in some way benefited from the sale of the defective product. For example, in drug and medical device litigation, liability may also extend to the physician or medical provider.

The Manufacturer

The manufacturer of the defective product is liable pursuant to all three primary theories of recovery, which include strict liability, negligence and breach of warranty. This rule applies not only to the manufacturer of the finished product, but to the manufacturer of any component of the finished product if that component was defective when it left the hands of the component manufacturer.

Product liability law no longer requires privity between the manufacturer and the plaintiff. The plaintiff must, however, be able to demonstrate a connection between the product and the manufacturer. In a minority of jurisdictions, privity of contract is still required in a breach of warranty claim.

The Retailer

The Restatement of Torts 2nd, Section 400, states:

> One who puts out as his own product a chattel manufactured by another is subject to the same liability as though he were the manufacturer.

Thus, under this section, strict liability would be available to an injured plaintiff against a retailer, who would otherwise not be strictly liable, when it sells a defective product. This rule would apply even if the seller lacked actual knowledge of the defect. An exclusion under this section applies if the actual manufacturer is clearly identified on the product.

This rule is a matter of public policy in that the public has a right to rely on the integrity of the seller, who is in a better position to put pressure on the manufacturer to provide safe products. Some jurisdictions have modified the general rule to exclude retailers under a strict liability theory when there is a solvent manufacturer who may be subject to a lawsuit in the jurisdiction.

Although all sellers in the distribution chain are theoretically liable, the retailer is not involved in the actual manufacturing of the product.

Thus, it would be difficult to find the retailer negligent in the manufacture of the product. Nevertheless, if the retailer undertakes inspecting or assembling the product before it is sold, it may be found liable for failure to take reasonable care in the course of such assembly or inspection.

The Seller of Used Products

A person who engages in buying or selling used products is generally not susceptible to strict liability because the chain of distribution has been broken. However, if the used seller does something intrusive with the product prior to sale, he or she may be held liable under a theory of secondary manufacture if what was done caused the defective condition.

This rule generally applies only if the seller is engaged in the regular practice of manufacturing, distributing or selling the particular type of product involved. Where the seller is not in the business of manufacturing or selling used products, but reconditions products for its own customers, it will not be held strictly liable, but may still be held liable for its own acts under a negligence theory.

The Assembler/Installer

A perfectly intact product may become defective if it is assembled or installed incorrectly. In general, this would confer the same liability upon the assembler/installer as it does upon the manufacturer or seller of the product. However, where the product was already in a defective state before it reached the hands of the assembler/installer, courts differ as to their imposition of strict liability. Liability may turn on the assembler/installer's ability to detect the defect during the assembly or installation.

The Physician or Medical Provider

In the area of drug and medical device litigation, the physician or medical provider may be held liable on the basis that they, as "learned intermediaries," have a duty to inform the patient of the risks of the products prescribed. This gives the patient the information he or she needs to make an informed decision about proceeding with the recommended course of therapy.

In general, the manufacturer of the drug or medical device relies on the physician or medical provider to adequately inform the patient based on the information given by the manufacturer to the physician concerning the particular drug or device. Of course, the manufacturer must supply the medical provider with adequate information on the known or foreseeable risks and hazards of the particular product. If it does not, it risks liability for its own negligence in providing inadequate warnings and instructions.

Product Liability Causes of Action

There are four main theories of liability which encompass a product liability claim: (1) Strict Liability; (2) Negligence; (3) Breach of Warranty; and (4) Intentional Tort.

Strict Liability

Strict liability refers to the liability of manufacturers for harm caused by their defective products, without any necessity for the plaintiff to prove fault on the part of the manufacturer. This elimination of fault was a monumental victory for consumers because it was often difficult to meet the fault standard of proof although the underlying claim was justified.

Further, the consumer is not in a position to detect a defect, nor should he or she bear the burden imposed when an injury results. It is the marketers of the product who are best able to bear the financial responsibility for injuries caused by their defective products, and adjust their costs accordingly. Thus, the issues in a strict liability claim are product-oriented.

Negligence

Negligence encompasses unintentionally caused harms, and is the most important basis of tort liability in the United States. The basis of liability is the creation of an unreasonable risk of harm to another. The product must involve a risk of harm greater than society is willing to accept in light of the benefits to be derived from that product—an unreasonable danger.

Unlike the strict liability claim, an analysis of the issues in a negligence claim are conduct-oriented. For example: Did the manufacturer adequately test the product before it was placed on the market? Did the manufacturer unreasonably cut corners when it chose to use a lower-grade metal that was more cost-efficient but produced a weaker foundation in a product? These are the types of issues that are presented to the jury in determining whether the conduct of the defendant was negligent.

In certain cases, the violation of a federal or state regulatory or statutory requirement concerning product quality may invoke the doctrine of negligence "per se." Negligence per se is the legal doctrine whereby certain acts are considered intrinsically negligent and thus there is a presumption of negligence, e.g., when the violation of a statute causes the type of injury that the statute was intended to prevent.

In determining whether the violation of a statute or regulation may be applied as proof of negligence, one must determine: (1) whether the injured person is within the class of persons who are protected by the statute; and (2) whether the particular injury suffered is the same injury the statute seeks to prevent. If the answer to both questions is yes, then the violation of that statute may constitute negligence per se.

Breach of Warranty

Breach of warranty is a claim which is more contractual than tortious— i.e., wrongful. There are three types of warranties upon which a consumer relies which may be violated: (1) Express Warranty; (2) Implied Warranty of Merchantability; and (3) Implied Warranty of Fitness for a Particular Purpose.

Express Warranty

An express warranty includes oral or written promises by the seller that the product will perform in a certain manner, or that the product conforms to its description. Under the law, an express warranty is defined as any affirmation of fact, description or sample furnished by the seller to the buyer that relates to the goods and becomes part of the basis of the bargain. Thus, it is "expressly warranted"—i.e., promised—that the product will conform to such affirmation, description or sample.

Further, it is not necessary that the warranty be reduced to writing, nor that any particular words be used, such as "guarantee," in order to create the obligation, as long as the representations were meant to be factual and not mere opinion. A thorough search of all product-related advertising, packaging and promotional items should be accomplished to either: (1) uncover and demonstrate the warranty on behalf of the plaintiff, or (2) in defense of the defendant, to show that there were no express warranties concerning the product.

Implied Warranty of Merchantability

An implied warranty of merchantability is an implied representation that the product is free of defects and meets the general standards of acceptability. Under the law, a warranty of merchantability is implied in a contract of sale if the seller is considered a merchant in the type of goods involved, unless the implied warranty is expressly excluded or modified by the seller.

Because a breach of implied warranty of merchantability results in an unacceptable product, it is unnecessary to prove reliance by the customer on either express or implied representations by the defendant. The unacceptable product itself forms the basis of the breach.

Implied Warranty of Fitness for a Particular Purpose

As the name demonstrates, this warranty includes the obligation that the product meets the needs of a particular purpose. Thus, although a product may be merchantable, it may still breach the implied warranty of fitness for a particular purpose if it is unfit for the purpose sought to be accomplished by the consumer.

Intentional Tort

An intentional tort differs from negligence in that—as the name implies—it requires the element of intent. In the context of product liability, the most common intentional tort would be fraudulent misrepresentation. For example, if a seller intentionally makes a material misrepresentation concerning the character or quality of the goods, and the purchaser justifiably relies on that misrepresentation, the seller is liable for physical harm resulting from the failure of the product to conform to the representation. [Restatement of Torts 2d, Section 402B].

CHAPTER 3:
THE CONSUMER
CREDIT PROTECTION ACT

IN GENERAL

The Consumer Credit Protection Act (PL 90-321, 1969) was enacted by Congress in 1968 to afford protection to the individual consumer in obtaining credit and managing debt. The Act consists of six subchapters that deal with various consumer credit issues, including:

Subchapter I: The Truth in Lending Act

Subchapter II: Garnishment Restrictions

Subchapter III: The Fair Credit Reporting Act

Subchapter IV: The Equal Credit Opportunity Act

Subchapter V: The Fair Debt Collection Practices Act

Subchapter VI: The Electronic Funds Transfer Act

SUBCHAPTER I: THE TRUTH IN LENDING ACT

Subchapter I of the Consumer Credit Protection Act deals with disclosure of the cost of consumer credit, and is known as the Truth in Lending Act (TILA).

The purpose of the TILA is

". . . to assure a meaningful disclosure of credit terms so that the consumer will be able to compare more readily the various credit terms available. . ."

The TILA preempts any state laws that are inconsistent with its disclosure provisions. Regulation "Z" refers to the Federal Reserve Board regulations that implement the TILA provisions.

Required Disclosure

Under the TILA, a consumer has the right to obtain complete and accurate information concerning a particular transaction before making a final decision. Sellers and creditors are obligated under state and federal laws to provide the consumer with this information. Every solicitation for credit must contain a brief disclosure statement setting forth the credit terms and conditions. More extensive disclosures are required with the application and following approval.

Disclosure must be made in writing and in a clear and conspicuous manner. Disclosure must be made in a timely manner so as to give the consumer a chance to consider them fully before entering into the transaction. In addition, specific disclosures concerning the finance charges and other fees must appear on the monthly billing statement.

Some of the terms and conditions the customer should inquire before entering into a credit transaction include the following:

1. How the payment is calculated;

2. The interest rate;

3. The annual percentage rate and whether it is fixed or variable;

4. The finance charge

5. The balance computation method

6. The grace period;

7. Transaction fees and charges, including overlimit fees, late fees, and the annual fee.

If a creditor violates the TILA disclosure provisions, it is liable to the consumer for actual damages. For example, an understatement of the finance charge may result in actual damages to the consumer computed as the difference between the finance charge as stated, and the finance charge as actually assessed. Nevertheless, if actual damages are not present, violations of the TILA still result in liability as set forth in the statute. Further, a consumer who prevails is generally entitled to legal fees expended in enforcing the statute.

Usury Laws

Many state laws provide that an individual cannot lend money at an interest rate that exceeds the state's statutory maximum—i.e., "the usury limit." "Usury" is generally defined as charging a price for credit that exceeds the usury limits set by law. Some states have no established usury limit. In addition, there are presently no federal usury limits.

The federal government relies on the Truth in Lending Act, which guarantees that lenders disclose their rates, fees and terms.

You may notice that your state has a reasonable usury limit, such as 12%, but your credit card carries an interest rate of 25%. The reason for this huge gap in permissible interest is that the interest rate assessed on your credit card is the rate established by the state in which the bank's credit card operations are situated. As long as the credit card issuer abides by the law of the state in which their credit card operations are located, the interest rates and fees they assess are legal, even if the consumer lives in a state that has a much lower usury limit. Most credit card issuers move their operations to the states that have these lender-friendly interest caps and few restrictions.

Therefore, it is advisable to take notice of the state in which the credit card operations for your credit cards are located, as this may indicate how high your credit card interest rates may rise, particularly if you make a late payment or otherwise default on your credit card agreement. Generally, credit card issuers include a provision in the credit agreement that allows them to raise your interest rate to their highest "default" rate if you fail to abide by any of the credit card terms, e.g. by exceeding your credit limit or making a late payment.

Presently, there are 26 states that have no limit on what bank credit card issuers can charge for interest rates, and 27 states have no limit on what they can charge for annual fees. California, Delaware, South Dakota and Tennessee have no set maximums on what they can charge for delinquency fees, cash advance fees, overlimit fees, transaction fees, ATM fees, etc., and do not provide any type of grace period. It is no coincidence that many credit cards are issued under the laws of those four states.

A table of state usury laws is set forth in Appendix 9.

The Minimum Payment Trap

Unfortunately, credit comes at a very costly price. As set forth above, interest rates can go as high as 30% or more, with additional fees and penalties tacked on for late payments, exceeding the credit limit, annual fees, etc. The result is that the average consumer can never pay off the principal balance, especially if he or she sticks to the minimum payment requested, keeping them forever in debt.

The average American household now has approximately $7,300 of credit card debt, and the average credit card interest rate is 16.75%. At this rate, it could take 44 years to pay off this credit card debt, and cost the consumer over $16,000 in interest if he or she continues to pay the minimum payment due, which many consumers choose to do.

Fortunately, 42% of credit card holders now pay off their balances in full each month, thus avoiding interest. Of course, credit card issuers are not happy when a credit card balance is paid off in full because it cuts into their profits.

Recognizing that paying the minimum payment requested on a credit card keeps the consumer indebted for many years, the Office of the Comptroller of Currency (OCC) instituted new rules regarding minimum credit card payments. The new rules went into full effect in 2005. Under the new rules, the minimum monthly payment amount for a credit card increased from 2% to 4% or more, depending on the bank that issued the credit card.

The minimum payment increase has been met with mixed reviews. Some consumers are unhappy that they have to increase their limited budget for credit card payments while others recognize that raising the minimum payment will help them pay down their debt much sooner.

Unauthorized Use of Credit Cards

The TILA was amended to virtually eliminate cardholder liability for the unauthorized use of credit cards. Under TILA, the cardholder is liable for its unauthorized use: (1) only if the card is an accepted card—i.e., not an unsolicited card; and (2) only to the extent of $50. Further, the unauthorized use of the credit card must occur before the cardholder has notified the card issuer that an unauthorized use has occurred or may occur as the result of loss or theft.

The card issuer must give adequate notice to the cardholder of the potential liability, and must provide the cardholder with a self-addressed stamped notice to be mailed by the cardholder in the event of loss or theft of the credit card. For the purposes of determining whether the card issuer has been properly notified, a cardholder notifies a card issuer by taking such steps as may be reasonably required in the ordinary course of business to provide the card issuer with the pertinent information whether or not the card issuer received this information.

This provision is not applicable in a situation where a cardholder voluntarily and knowingly allows another person to use his credit card and that other person subsequently misuses the card. Unauthorized use of a credit card occurs only where there is no actual, implied, or apparent authority for such use by the cardholder.

In any action by a card issuer to enforce liability for the unauthorized use of a credit card, the burden of proof is on the card issuer to show that the use was authorized, or that the conditions of liability for the unauthorized use have been met.

Unauthorized Use Defined

TILA defines "unauthorized use" as "use by a person other than the cardholder who does not have actual, implied or apparent authority for such use, and from which the cardholder receives no benefit." The statute does not define the meaning of "actual, implied or apparent authority." According to the Federal Reserve Board—the entity responsible for interpreting TILA and its regulations—whether actual, implied or apparent authority exists is to be determined under state or other applicable law.

While it is clear that unauthorized use of another's credit card by a finder or a thief is the intention and meaning of the statute, it is less clear whether unauthorized use includes use by another who initially was authorized, but whom the cardholder no longer authorizes to use the credit card.

Limiting Your Financial Damages

In order to limit your financial damages from the loss, theft and unauthorized use of your credit card, you must notify the card issuer as quickly as possible. Many companies operate a 24-hour toll-free number for cardholders to report lost and stolen credit cards. It is advisable to follow up with a letter. Include the following information: (1) your account number; (2) the date you noticed your card was missing; and (3) the date you first reported the loss. Send the letter by certified mail, return receipt requested, and keep a copy of the letter and the mailing receipt in a safe place until the problem is resolved to your satisfaction.

In addition to reporting your credit card loss or theft, you should review your subsequent billing statements carefully. If your statements show any unauthorized charges, you must send a letter to the credit card issuer describing each questionable charge. Again, advise the card issuer of the date your card was lost or stolen, and when you first notified them of the loss or theft. Enclose a copy of your notification letter. Send your follow-up letter to the address provided for billing errors. Again, send the letter by certified mail, return receipt requested, and keep a copy of the letter and the mailing receipt in a safe place until the problem is resolved.

Under the Fair Credit Billing Act (FCBA), which is further discussed below, if you report the loss before the credit card is used, the FCBA provides that the card issuer cannot hold you responsible for any unauthorized charges. If a finder or thief uses your cards before you report them missing, the most you will owe for unauthorized charges is $50 per card. This is true even if a finder or thief uses your credit card at an ATM machine to access your credit card account.

SUBCHAPTER II: GARNISHMENT RESTRICTIONS

Restrictions on garnishment were enacted as Subchapter II of the Consumer Credit Protection Act to: (1) protect the consumer from having an excessive number of garnishments placed on his or her income as a result of indebtedness; and (2) prevent the consumer from being discharged by their employers due to a wage garnishment.

Limit on Amount Garnished

The law limits the amount of an employee's earnings which may be garnished in any one work week or pay period to the lesser of 25% of disposable earning—the amount of employee earnings left after legally required deductions have been made for federal, state and local taxes, social security, unemployment insurance and state employee retirement systems—or the amount by which disposable earnings are greater than 30 times the federal minimum hourly wage prescribed by section 6(a)(1) of the Fair Labor Standards Act of 1938. Other deductions that are not required by law, e.g., union dues, health and life insurance, and charitable contributions, are not subtracted from gross earnings when calculating the amount of disposable earnings for garnishment purposes.

In court orders for child support or alimony, the law allows up to 50% of an employee's disposable earnings to be garnished if the employee is supporting a spouse or child, and up to 60% for an employee who is not. An additional 5% may be garnished for support payments that are more than 12 weeks in arrears. Such garnishments are not subject to the restrictions noted in the preceding paragraph.

Garnishment restrictions do not apply to bankruptcy court orders and debts due for federal and state taxes. In addition, the Act does not affect voluntary wage assignments—i.e., situations in which workers voluntarily agree that their employers may turn over some specified amount of their earnings to a creditor.

Subsequent Wage Garnishments

The federally-mandated 25% limitation on a wage garnishment applies to the maximum amount that can be garnished by all of the debtor's ordinary creditors, not just one. Thus, if a debtor is already subject to another garnishment, their wages cannot be garnished further by a subsequent garnishment unless:

1. The first garnishment takes less than 25% of the debtor's disposable income, or

2. The garnishment is for alimony or child support.

Employer Violations

If an employer violates Title III, he may be subject to certain penalties, such as reinstatement of a discharged employee with back pay, and the restoration of improperly garnished amounts. Where violations cannot be resolved through informal means, court action may be initiated to restrain and remedy violations. Employers who willfully violate the law may be prosecuted criminally and fined up to $1,000, or imprisoned for not more than one year, or both.

SUBCHAPTER III: THE FAIR CREDIT REPORTING ACT

Limited Right to Access Consumer Credit Report

Under the FCRA, creditors may only obtain a consumer's credit report for limited purposes, the most common of which are extension of credit or employment. In addition, a creditor may only request a credit report for the individual consumer involved in the transaction, and cannot obtain a spouse's credit report if the spouse is not a party to the transaction. It is a crime under the FCRA to obtain a consumer's credit report under false pretenses.

If the credit reporting agency willfully or negligently issues a report to a person who does not have a permissible purpose in obtaining the report, the agency is subject to civil liability. An individual credit reporting agency employee who knowingly and willingly issues the report may be subject to criminal sanctions.

Duty to Maintain Accurate Information

The FCRA also requires credit reporting agencies to maintain accurate information, and to permit consumers to correct any inaccuracies found in their reports. However, a credit reporting agency is not subject to civil liability for inaccuracies contained in consumer credit reports provided they "follow reasonable procedures to assure maximum possible accuracy of the information. . .". Nevertheless, if the credit-reporting agency does not follow "reasonable procedures," they may be subject to liability.

When reviewing your credit report, make sure all of your personal information is correct, including your name, address, social security number, date of birth, employer, etc. Sometimes credit data get placed on the wrong report, especially if you have a common name, e.g. Mary Jones. This often happens with family members who have the same name, such as John Smith, Sr. and John Smith, Jr.

You should dispute erroneous negative information in your credit report immediately. If a consumer disputes the accuracy of information contained in his or her file, the credit reporting agency is required to reinvestigate this information within a reasonable period of time. If, upon reinvestigation, the information cannot be verified, or is proven inaccurate, it must be deleted, and corrected copies must be sent to all parties who recently requested copies of the report.

If an item is changed or removed as a result of your dispute, the credit reporting agency cannot put the disputed information back in your file unless the information provider verifies its accuracy and completeness. If reinvestigation does not resolve your dispute with the credit reporting agency, you are entitled to include your statement of the dispute in your file and in future reports. Upon your request, the credit reporting agency will provide your statement to anyone who received a copy of the old report in the recent past for a fee.

A sample notification letter disputing erroneous information is set forth in Appendix 10.

Remedies

A credit reporting agency is liable to the consumer for any actual damages suffered as a result of negligence. Actual damages generally include monetary losses and have also been held to include damages for mental anguish resulting from aggravation, embarrassment, humiliation and injury to reputation, etc. Further, if the violation is willful, punitive damages may also be available to the consumer.

Contact information for the three major national credit reporting agencies is as follows:

EQUIFAX
P.O. Box 740241
Atlanta, GA 30374
Tel: (800) 685-1111
Website: www.equifax.com

EXPERIAN
701 Experian Parkway
Allen, TX 75013
Tel: (888) 397-3742
Website: www.experian.com

TRANS UNION
P.O. Box 1000
Chester, PA 19022
Tel: (800) 916-8800
Website: www.transunion.com

The Fair and Accurate Credit Transactions Act

Under the Fair and Accurate Credit Transactions (FACT) Act of 2003, a consumer is entitled to receive a free copy of their consumer disclosure every 12 months from all three major credit reporting agencies listed above. A consumer disclosure refers to all the information in a consumer's credit report that the credit reporting agencies maintain. A consumer disclosure differs from a credit report in that a credit report contains only some of the information in the consumer's credit file.

Under the FACT Act, you are also entitled to receive this information at no charge if you certify to the credit reporting agency that:

1. You are unemployed and intend to apply for employment in the 60-day period beginning on the date you make the certification;

2. You receive public welfare assistance;

3. You believe your file contains inaccurate information due to fraud; or

4. You are a victim of identity theft.

You can request your FACT Act consumer disclosure from one or more of the three credit reporting agencies online, by telephone and by mail, as follows:

Online: Access the website at http://www.annualcreditreport.com/. Follow the instructions on the website.

By Telephone: Call 1-877-322-8228 to request your credit reports by phone. You will go through a simple verification process over the phone, and your reports will be mailed to you.

By Mail: Send your request to the following address:

Annual Credit Report Request Service
P.O. Box 105281
Atlanta, GA 30348-5281

An annual credit report request form is set forth in Appendix 11.

SUBCHAPTER IV: THE EQUAL CREDIT OPPORTUNITY ACT

Due to concerns that the issuance of credit could be a source of discrimination, and that all individuals would not have equal access to credit, the Equal Credit Opportunity Act (ECOA) was enacted in 1972. The ECOA requires that all credit applicants be considered on the basis of their actual qualifications for credit and not be rejected because of certain personal characteristics including: (1) gender; (2) race; (3) marital status; (4) religion; (5) national origin; (6) age; or (7) receipt of public income.

Except for religion, creditors may ask for this information in certain situations, but they may not use it to discriminate against an individual when deciding whether to grant credit. In addition, you cannot be denied credit because you exercised your rights under Federal credit laws such as filing a billing error notice with a creditor pursuant to the Fair Credit Billing Act.

There are factors, however, a creditor can legally consider in their decision. For example, a creditor can consider any factors that shed light on your creditworthiness. Those factors include: (1) Capacity—your ability to repay the debt; (2) Character—your willingness to repay the debt; and (3) Collateral—your security for the debt.

Under the ECOA, you must be notified within 30 days after your application has been completed whether you have been approved or not. If credit is denied, this notice must be in writing and it must explain the specific reasons why you were denied credit or tell you of your right to ask for an explanation. You have the same rights if an account you have had is closed.

If you are denied credit, you should find out why. There may be an error or the computer system may not have evaluated all relevant information. In that case, you can ask the creditor to reconsider your application. The creditor must give you a notice that tells you either the specific reasons for your rejection or your right to learn the reasons, provided you make the request within 60 days of the denial.

If you think you have been discriminated against, cite the law to the lender. If the lender still refuses without a satisfactory explanation, you may contact a federal enforcement agency for assistance or bring legal action. You can also check with your state Attorney General to see if the creditor violated state equal credit opportunity laws. Your state may decide to prosecute the creditor.

If you're denied credit, the creditor must give you the name and address of the agency that regulates that particular creditor. While some of these agencies don't resolve individual complaints, the information you provide helps them decide which companies to investigate. Your complaint letter should state the facts. Send it, along with copies—not originals—of supporting documents.

SUBCHAPTER V: THE FAIR DEBT COLLECTION PRACTICES ACT

In 1988, the Fair Debt Collection Practices Act (FDCPA) was enacted as Subchapter V of the Consumer Credit Protection Act to supplement the statutory and common law tort remedies available to the debtor to restrain unfair debt collection procedures. The Act contains detailed provisions regulating the manner in which debt collection is carried out. Many state debt collection harassment statutes are patterned after the Fair Debt Collection Practices Act (FDCPA). The FDCPA applies only to debt collection agencies whereas the state statutes modeled after the Act generally apply to creditors as well. Attorneys are not included in the definition of debt collector under the Act.

A table of state debt collection statutes is set forth in Appendix 12.

The FDCPA requires debt collectors to provide information about the alleged debt, and verification of the debt, at the request of the consumer, including the name of the creditor, the amount of the debt, and an offer to provide the name of the original creditor, if different. In addition, a statement must be sent, generally with the first communication, advising the debtor that the debt will be assumed valid if he or she fails to dispute its validity within 30 days. If the debtor disputes the validity of the debt, the debt collector must verify the debt with the creditor.

A debt collector may not contact the debtor if, within 30 days after the debtor receives written notice of the debt, they send the collection agency a letter stating they do not owe the money. However, a collector can renew collection activities if they send proof of the debt, such as a copy of a bill for the amount owed. A debt collector may not apply a payment to any debt the debtor believes they do not owe. If the debtor owes more than one debt, any payment they make must be applied to the debt they indicate as valid.

Prohibited Collection Practices

The Fair Debt Collection Practices Act prohibits various kinds of collection practices, including, but not limited to:

1. Communicating with the debtor at an unusual or inconvenient time or place;

2. Communicating with the debtor at his or her place of employment if the employer prohibits such communications, or if the debtor requests that he or she not be contacted there;

3. Communicating with a debtor who is represented by an attorney;

4. Communicating with third parties without the authorization of the debtor;

5. Communicating with the debtor after he or she has notified the debt collector to cease communication concerning the debt. In this case, the debt collector may not contact the debtor except for the limited purpose of advising the debtor, in writing, of further action to be taken;

6. Making false, deceptive or misleading representations;

7. Using unfair or unconscionable conduct to collect the debt; and

8. Using harassing, threatening or otherwise abusive conduct to collect the debt.

In addition, if the debtor has an attorney, the debt collector must contact the attorney, rather than the debtor. If the debtor does not have an attorney, a collector may contact other people, but only to find out the debtor's address, telephone number, and place of employment. Debt collectors are usually prohibited from contacting third parties more than once. In most cases, the collector may not tell anyone other than the debtor and their attorney that the debtor owes money.

Remedies

If a debt collector violates any of the provisions of the Fair Debt Collection Practices Act, he or she is liable to the person with whom the violation took place. This would include the debtor and any other persons who were subject to the debt collector's improper tactics. The statute of limitations—the time period within which the action must be commenced—is one year under the Act. A statute of limitations refers to the period within which an action must be commenced by law. Different types of actions carry different time periods.

The debtor is entitled to actual damages, including physical or emotional injury, and actual expenses. The debtor is also entitled to statutory damages of up to One Thousand ($1,000.00) Dollars as set forth in the Act, whether or not actual damages exist, and whether or not the violation was intentional or inadvertent. Debtors who prevail on their claim may also be entitled to legal fees and costs at the discretion of the court.

SUBCHAPTER VI: THE ELECTRONIC FUNDS TRANSFER ACT

The Electronic Funds Transfer Act (the "EFTA") was enacted as Subchapter VI of the Consumer Credit Protection Act for the purpose of providing a basic framework establishing the rights, liabilities, and responsibilities of participants in electronic fund transfer systems. The EFTA provides consumers protection for all transactions using a debit card, ATM card, or other electronic means to debit or credit a consumer's bank account. The EFTA also limits a consumer's liability for unauthorized electronic fund transfers.

The EFTA is discussed more fully in Chapter 4 (Consumer Banking) of this Almanac.

THE FAIR CREDIT BILLING ACT

Correcting Billing Errors

The Fair Credit Billing Act (FCBA) establishes procedures for correcting billing errors. The law applies to "open end" credit accounts such as credit cards and revolving charge accounts. Under the law, card issuers must follow the rules for promptly correcting any billing errors, including:

1. Unauthorized charges;

2. Incorrect charges;

3. Math errors;

4. Failure to post payments and credits;

5. Failure to provide bills; and

6. Charges for which the cardholder has requested an explanation or written proof of purchase or clarification.

Most creditors do not provide copies of sales receipts with the monthly statement. The statement merely lists the merchant name, and the date and amount of the purchase. Therefore, the cardholder is advised to keep all of their sales receipts in order to check them against the statement to determine whether there has been a billing error.

If the cardholder suspects that there is a billing error, he or she must notify the card issuer, in writing, at the address specified for billing errors. This address usually appears on the billing statement. This notification must be made within 60 days after the first bill containing the error was mailed to the customer. Therefore, it is important for cardholders to review their credit card billing statements as soon as possible after receipt.

The billing error notification letter should include the name of the cardholder, the account number, the suspected error, the amount in dispute, and the reason why the cardholder believes the charge is in error. Include copies—not originals—of any documentation that supports the dispute, such as sales receipts. The letter should be sent by certified mail, return receipt requested, so there is proof of mailing. A copy of the letter and proof of mailing should be kept in a safe place until the dispute is resolved.

A sample notification of billing error is set forth in Appendix 13.

The law requires the card issuer to acknowledge the cardholder's letter within 30 days unless the card issuer corrects the billing error in less time. The card issuer is also required to investigate the error and either correct it or provide an explanation as to why they believe no error has been made. The card issuer has up to two billing periods, but no more than 90 days to respond.

A creditor who violates the rules for the correction of billing errors automatically loses the amount owed on the item in question and any finance charges on it, up to a combined total of $50 even if the bill was correct. The cardholder may also sue for actual damages plus twice the amount of any finance charges. The amount sought as damages must be a minimum of $100 up to a maximum of $1,000. The cardholder is also entitled to court costs and attorney's fees if the lawsuit is successful. A class action lawsuit—one filed on behalf of a group of people with similar claims—is also permitted under the law.

During the investigation period, the cardholder is entitled to withhold payment on the disputed amount while the error is being investigated. The card issuer cannot demand that the cardholder pay the disputed amount or any related finance charges or fees while the investigation is ongoing. In addition, the card issuer cannot report the account as delinquent. The card issuer is required to correct the error promptly without damaging the cardholder's credit record. Until the card issuer responds to the problem, the law forbids it from taking any collection action of the disputed amount.

The cardholder must, however, still pay any part of the bill that is not in dispute, including finance and other charges. However, in order to take advantage of this protection, the cardholder must comply with the 60-day notification period discussed above.

If it is subsequently determined that there was no billing error, the card issuer is entitled to reinstate the charge, including any finance charges that accumulated and any minimum payments missed while the charge was being investigated. If the cardholder fails to pay the disputed amount at that point, the card issuer may then take legal action to collect the amount due and may report the overdue payment to a credit bureau.

If the cardholder continues to dispute the charge, the card issuer must report to the credit bureau that the cardholder has challenged the bill, and give the cardholder written notice of the name and address of each person who has received information about the dispute. If and when the dispute is resolved, the outcome must again be reported to each person who has received information about the account.

Disputed Transactions

In addition to regulating billing errors, the Fair Credit Billing Act also assists cardholders who have a dispute with a merchant concerning merchandise or services that were charged to their credit card. If the cardholder has not already paid off the balance, the law allows the cardholder to withhold payment that is still due for the disputed transaction, provided the cardholder has made a genuine attempt to solve the problem with the merchant. The cardholder can withhold payment up to the amount of credit outstanding for the purchase, plus any finance or related charges.

If the card used to make the purchase was a bank credit card, or a travel and entertainment card, or another card not issued by the merchant, the above protections still apply, however, the cardholder can withhold payment only if the purchase exceeded $50 and occurred in the cardholder's home state or within 100 miles of their billing address.

RESOLVING YOUR CREDIT COMPLAINT

If you are having a credit problem covered by federal law, you should first try to solve the problem directly with creditor or other financial institution with whom you conduct business. If you are unable to resolve your problem at this level, you may file a written complaint with the Federal agency responsible for enforcing consumer credit protection laws, as set forth below.

State-Chartered Banks

If you have a complaint about a bank or other financial institution, you may file a written complaint with the Federal Reserve System. The Federal Reserve System investigates consumer complaints received against state-chartered banks that are members of the Federal Reserve System. Complaints about state-chartered banks are investigated by one of the 12 Federal Reserve Banks around the country. Complaints about other financial institutions are referred to the appropriate federal regulatory agency.

You should submit your written complaint to Federal Reserve in care of the following address:

Division of Consumer and Community Affairs,

Board of Governors of the Federal Reserve System,

Washington, D.C. 20551

In your written complaint, you should include the complete name and address of the bank, a brief description of your complaint, and copies—not originals—of any documentation that will support your complaint. The Federal Reserve will generally respond to your written complaint within 15 business days, and advise you whether the Federal Reserve will investigate your complaint or whether your complaint will be forwarded to another federal agency.

If the Federal Reserve handles the investigation, it will analyze the bank's response to your complaint to ensure that your concerns have been addressed, and will send you a follow-up letter discussing their findings. If the investigation reveals that a Federal Reserve regulation has been violated, you will be advised of the violation and the corrective action the bank has been directed to take.

Although the Federal Reserve investigates all complaints about the banks it regulates, it does not have the authority to resolve all types of problems, such as contractual or factual disputes of disagreements about bank policies or procedures. In many instances, however, if you file a complaint, a bank may voluntarily work with you to resolve your situation. If the matter is not resolved, you will be advised whether you should consider legal counsel to handle your complaint.

National Banks

File a complaint with the Office of the Comptroller of the Currency, Compliance Management, Mail Stop 7-5, Washington, D.C. 20219.

Federal Credit Unions

File a complaint with the National Credit Union Administration, 1776 G St., N.W., Washington, D.C. 20456.

Non-Member Federally Insured Banks

File a complaint with the Office of Consumer Programs, Federal Deposit Insurance Corporation, 550 Seventeenth St., N.W., Washington, D.C. 20429.

Federally Insured Savings and Loans, and Federally Chartered State Banks

File a complaint with the Consumer Affairs Program, Office of Thrift Supervision, 1700 G St., N.W., Washington, D.C. 20552.

CHAPTER 4:
CONSUMER BANKING

IN GENERAL

Every consumer at one time or another has contact with or develops a relationship with a bank, whether through a checking account, savings account, mortgage, car loan, business loan, investments, or other financial matter. The customer encounters many issues in its dealings with a bank, some complex and some simple, and thus should be well-informed about their rights and responsibilities. The banking industry is highly regulated, and is subject to both federal and state statutes designed to protect the consumer.

SHOPPING FOR A BANK

Selecting a bank to use for your financial affairs is a very important decision. One should take time to research the prospective bank before making a decision. Visit the branch you intend to use to do your banking. Ask questions. Is the staff knowledgeable, courteous and helpful? Were you given complete and satisfactory information concerning prospective products and services? If not, it is best to do your banking elsewhere to avoid future problems.

NEW PROOF OF IDENTITY REQUIREMENT UNDER USA PATRIOT ACT

The U.S. Treasury Department and federal financial regulatory agencies have jointly issued new rules for customer identification pursuant to the USA Patriot Act of 2001. Under the new rules, which became mandatory on October 1, 2003, financial institutions are required to ask customers for proof of their name, address, date of birth, and social security number when opening a new account. Documentation, such as a driver's license or passport, must be provided for verification.

Identification procedures may vary depending upon the type of account being opened and the policies of the financial institution. The financial institution must also check the customer's name to see whether it appears on any list of suspected terrorists or terrorist organizations. The new rules are in effect to prevent crimes such as money laundering, identity theft, and account fraud, that have been known to be a source of funds for terrorist operations.

TYPES OF BANK ACCOUNTS

The most common types of bank accounts used by the average customer are the savings account and the checking account. Both types of accounts may provide for the payment of interest to the depositor.

Savings Account

Savings accounts are governed by the federal Truth in Savings Act. Under the Truth in Savings Act, financial institutions are required to:

1. Disclose the Annual Percentage Yield (the "APY") on savings accounts.

2. Credit the entire deposit instead of crediting a portion of the deposit.

3. Refrain from advertising "free checking" with the savings account if there are any hidden charges or requirements, such as maintaining a minimum balance in the account to qualify.

Checking Account

Banks generally have a wide range of checking account types. Before opening an account, the customer should inquire about the various fees and obligations applicable to each type of checking account. One should consider which type of account meets their individual needs.

One factor to consider may be the number of checks the customer intends to write per month. Some banks offer low or no-fee checking, however, the customer can only write a limited number of checks from the account during the statement period. If the customer exceeds that number, additional charges may apply. If the customer regularly writes a large number of checks, he or she may prefer the type of account that charges a higher monthly fee, but permits unlimited check writing privileges.

SAFE DEPOSIT BOXES

One of the services a bank offers its customers is the ability to rent a safe deposit box. Most customers who rent safe deposit boxes do so in order to have a secure place to keep valuables and important documents. Also, some insurance companies charge lower insurance premiums on valuables kept in a bank's safe deposit box instead of at home.

The bank is treated as the bailee—i.e.., a safekeeper—of the safe deposit box. The bank may limit the persons who have access to the box, and the hours they may gain access. Most banks have very strict safe deposit box access procedures, e.g., signature verification, restricted access, dual key access, etc. In addition, customers are not left unattended inside the vault, but are directed to viewing rooms outside of the vault where they can inspect their property in privacy.

Items You Should Place in a Safety Deposit Box

There are certain valuable items and important documents which one may want to place in a safe deposit box. These may include originals insurance policies; family records such as birth, marriage and death certificates; original deeds, titles, mortgages, leases and other contracts; stocks, bonds and certificates of deposit (CDs); valuable jewels, medals, rare stamps and other collectibles, negatives for irreplaceable photos, and videos or pictures of your home's contents for insurance purposes, in case of theft or damage.

Items You Should Not Place in a Safety Deposit Box

There are certain items which should not be placed in a safe deposit box. For example, any item one may need in an emergency should not be in the safe deposit box, such as passports; medical care directives, e.g., a health care proxy; and funeral or burial instructions.

In addition, it is not advisable to have one's will located in the safe deposit box unless someone other than the customer has access to the box in case the customer dies. For example, if you choose to put your will in the safe deposit box, the person designated to oversee your financial affairs should have immediate access to the original will. Otherwise, some states will require a court order to open the safe deposit box, which can cause unnecessary time and expense.

The customer can jointly rent the box with a spouse, child or other person who will have unrestricted access to the box. It is not enough to merely give someone a key to the box because the bank may not allow them access, under state, law, if they are not a joint-renter.

Insurance

FDIC Insurance does not cover the contents of safe deposit boxes if they are damaged or stolen. By law, the FDIC only insures deposits in deposit accounts at insured institutions. Even though the customer is technically "depositing" valuables, including cash and checks, into the safe deposit box, these are not deposits under the insurance laws. A safe deposit box is strictly a storage space provided by the bank.

It is possible that the contents of the safe deposit box may be covered under homeowner's insurance, therefore, the customer should check his or her policy to determine whether coverage is available. The customer should keep a log of everything that is contained in the box, as well as photographs of any valuables, in case an item is lost and an insurance claim needs to be filed.

The bank would only be liable for damage or loss of the safe deposit box if it was negligent in the way it handled or protected the box. Because safe deposit boxes are stored in concrete and steel vaults with sophisticated security equipment, it is unlikely that a safe deposit box would be stolen. In addition, in order to gain access to the box, most banks have strict access procedures, discussed above.

Further Safeguards

The customer should take additional steps to make sure their valuables are protected. The customer is generally given two keys to the safe deposit box. The keys to the box should be kept in a safe place, apart from each other, and apart from the house keys and car keys, and should not indicate the name of the bank where the box is located. If one of the keys is lost, the bank should be notified so they can be on alert in case someone tries to use the key. If both keys are lost, the customer will have to get a new box.

When visiting the bank, accompany the bank employee into the vault while he or she opens and closes the safe deposit box door with the key. Do not permit the bank employee to take the box out of your sight. Never leave the key in the box door. Do not open the box until you are alone in the privacy of the viewing area. Before leaving this area, make sure all valuables are returned to the box. When you return the box to the vault, make sure the box door is locked and take your key.

Abandonment of Property

If the customer does not pay the fee after a certain time period, as determined by state law, and the bank is unable to locate the customer, the safe deposit box may be declared abandoned and the contents turned over to the state's unclaimed property office. This may occur if the customer dies and nobody is aware that he or she had a safe deposit box.

SWITCHING BANKS

For a number of reasons, a customer may wish to switch banks, e.g., if they are moving, or if another bank is offering a better deal. In order to make sure that the change goes smoothly, the following steps should be followed:

1. The existing checkbook should be balanced and all outstanding checks should have cleared before the checking account is closed. This will ensure that no checks will be presented after the account is closed, resulting in unnecessary fees.

2. Open an account at the new bank before leaving the old bank so that you can continue banking activities, e.g. writing checks, etc., without interruption.

3. If your checks are being directly deposited, do not close the old account until you have confirmed that the direct deposits are being made to the new account.

4. If automatic payments are being made from the old account, e.g., to pay monthly bills, confirm when the payments will start being made from the new account before closing the old account.

5. If you are moving, give the old bank your new contact information, in writing, in case they need to reach you regarding your closed account.

6. Make a notation in your financial records that the old account was closed, and the date on which it was closed, so that individuals investigating your financial affairs in the future, e.g., heirs, will not waste time trying to track down a closed account.

7. Make sure any safe deposit box held at the bank is emptied and the keys returned to the bank.

MAINTAINING BANK RECORDS

It is important to keep careful financial records for a number of reasons. For example, federal tax rules require an individual to maintain receipts and other financial documents that support items on a tax return for as long as the IRS can assess additional taxes—e.g., up to three years from the date the tax return was filed and, in some cases, up to six years. The following items should be kept in a safe place for a reasonable period of time:

1. Canceled Checks - Checks that support tax return items, such as charitable contributions, should be held for at least seven years. Checks with no long-term significance should be held for approximately one year. Checks, receipts and documents relating to large purchases, such as the purchase of a home or car, should be kept indefinitely.

2. Transaction Receipts - Receipts for deposits, and ATM, debit and credit card transactions should be kept until the information appears on the statement and has been verified.

3. Bank Account Statements - Bank statements should be kept for up to seven years, e.g., for tax purposes.

4. Loan Documents - Loan documents should be kept for as long as the account is open.

5. Investment Statements - Documentation of the purchase or sale of stocks, bonds and other investments should be kept as long as the investment property is owned, and for seven years after the property has been sold or transferred, e.g., for tax purposes.

FORGOTTEN ASSETS

Old family documents often contain evidence of bank accounts, safe deposit boxes and other investments. The FDIC receives many phone calls from people trying to find out information about old accounts. In most cases, the accounts had been closed long ago. However, occasionally, abandoned or forgotten assets are in the custody of the bank, a state government or the FDIC. If evidence of an old account or safe deposit box is discovered, one must first determine whether the financial institution is still in business. If the financial institution is still open, request a status report on the old accounts. If the account was not closed by the original owner, it is possible that the assets may still be available from the bank, or the assets may have been deemed abandoned and transferred to the state's unclaimed property office.

If a state has funds, and the individual provides satisfactory proof of ownership, the funds will be released. Even if a state has already sold an asset, the original owner or heirs generally have the right to claim the proceeds from the sale. If the bank was closed by the government, the deposits and safe deposit boxes may have been transferred to another institution or to the FDIC. In most cases, there is an acquiring institution for the failed bank's deposits and safe deposit boxes.

DEBIT AND ATM CARDS

A debit or ATM card is linked to the cardholder's bank account. Although these cards are used in much the same way as an ordinary credit card, the cost of anything purchased, or money withdrawn from a bank automatic teller machine (ATM), will be deducted from the cardholder's bank account immediately. Thus, these cards effectively replace cash and checks, and reduce a bank's processing costs.

The ATM card is used at establishments that accept the ATM card as payment for goods and services, and at bank ATMs that accept the ATM card to withdraw money from the cardholder's bank account. When using an ATM card, the cardholder is generally required to enter their personal identification number (PIN) to complete the purchase.

The debit card, unlike an ordinary ATM card, usually carries the logos of one of the two major credit card companies—VISA or MasterCard, e.g., a "debit Visa" or a "debit MasterCard." The debit card can be used to make purchases anywhere the logos on these cards are accepted. When using the debit card for purchases, the cardholder is not required to enter their PIN number to complete the purchase. Debit cards are a convenient way for those persons who do not qualify for a credit card to make purchases without using checks or having to carry a large amount of cash.

Most banks do not charge any fees for making purchases with a debit or ATM card. The purchases and ATM withdrawals are listed on the customer's monthly banking statement so they can track their spending and make sure there are no fraudulent transactions on the account. This is particularly important because, unlike a credit card where the bank suffers the loss incurred by fraudulent activity, when someone uses a debit card, the funds are immediately withdrawn from the cardholder's bank account. This could cause bounced checks, overdraft charges, etc., which may be very difficult to sort out and correct.

The Electronic Funds Transfer Act

The Electronic Fund Transfer Act (EFTA) provides consumers protection for all transactions using a debit card, ATM card, or other electronic means to debit or credit a consumer's bank account. The EFTA also limits a consumer's liability for unauthorized electronic fund transfers. Electronic funds transfer systems under the EFTA include:

1. Automated Teller Machines;

2. Pay-by-Phone services;

3. Direct Deposit and Automatic Payment services; and

4. Point of Sale Transfer systems, which permit a consumer to pay for goods and services by transferring funds simultaneously out of the consumer's bank account and into the seller's account at the time of purchase, e.g., using a debit or ATM card.

Resolving Disputes

Under the EFTA, procedures have been established for resolving errors on bank account statements, including: (1) Electronic fund transfers that the consumer did not make; (2) Electronic fund transfers that are incorrectly identified or show the wrong amount or date; (3) Computation or similar errors; (4) The failure to properly reflect payments, credits, or electronic fund transfers; and (5) Electronic fund transfers for which the consumer requests an explanation or documentation, because of a possible error.

Under the EFTA, if there is a mistake or unauthorized withdrawal from your bank account through the use of a debit card, ATM card, or other electronic fund transfer, you must notify your bank of the problem or error not later than 60 days after the statement containing the problem or error was sent. Although most banks have a toll-free number to report the problem, you should follow up in writing.

For retail purchases, your bank has up to 10 business days to investigate after receiving your notice of the error. The bank must tell you the results of its investigation within 3 business days of completing its investigation. The error must be corrected within 1 business day after determining the error has occurred. If the bank needs more time, it may take up to 90 days to complete the investigation, but only if it returns the money in dispute to the customer's account within 10 business days after receiving notice of the error.

Under the EFTA, there are three levels of liability that may be assessed against the consumer for unauthorized transfers.

1. If an unauthorized withdrawal is made from the consumer's bank account prior to the consumer being aware that his or her access card was lost or stolen, the consumer may be held liable for amounts withdrawn from the consumer's bank account prior to his or her notification to the bank, up to a maximum of $50.00.

2. If the consumer fails to notify the bank that his or her access card was lost or stolen within two business days of the consumer being aware of the loss, the consumer may be held liable for amounts withdrawn from the consumer's bank account prior to his or her notification to the bank, up to a maximum of $500.00.

3. If the consumer fails to report unauthorized transfers within 60 days of receiving a statement on which the unauthorized transfer appears, the consumer may have unlimited liability for amounts withdrawn from the consumer's bank account prior to his or her notification to the bank. That means the consumer could lose all the money in their bank account and the unused portion of their maximum line of credit established for overdrafts. The rationale for this apparently harsh rule is that the consumer would have to be unduly negligent for failing to notify the bank within that time period.

Some banks may voluntarily cap a consumer's liability at $50 for certain types of transactions, regardless of when they report the loss or theft. However, because this protection is offered voluntarily, the policies could change at any time. Thus, the consumer is advised to ask their bank about its liability limits.

Remedies

If your bank does not follow the provisions of the EFTA, you may sue for actual damages—and in some cases, three times actual damages— plus punitive damages of not less than $100 nor more than $1,000. You are also entitled to court costs and attorney's fees in a successful lawsuit. Class action suits are also permitted. If the institution fails to make an electronic fund transfer, or to stop payment of a preauthorized transfer when properly instructed by you to do so, you may sue for all damages that result from the failure.

Lost or Stolen Debit or ATM Card

If your debit or ATM card is lost or stolen, you must immediately report the loss to the bank that issued the card in order to limit your liability for unauthorized use. There are certain laws that protect a debit or ATM cardholder from liability if the card is lost or stolen. Under the EFTA, if the cardholder reports the loss to the issuer 2 business days after they discover that the card is missing, their losses are limited to a maximum of $50 for any unauthorized use.

If the cardholder waits more than two business days to report the loss or theft, they are potentially responsible for any additional amounts resulting from their failure to notify the card issuer—up to $500. If the cardholder does not report the loss or theft within 60 days after receiving a bank statement that includes an unauthorized transfer, the law doesn't require the bank to reimburse the customer for any losses due to unauthorized transfers made after that 60-day period. Thus, the cardholder may be responsible for unlimited loss on transactions that occurred after the 60-day period.

Nevertheless, depending on the circumstances, if it is clear that the cardholder is an innocent victim of fraud, and he or she promptly reports the loss or theft of the card, or an unauthorized transaction, many banks will voluntarily hold the customer to no liability. The bank may ask the cardholder to sign an affidavit or other notice of the loss or theft.

For the above reasons, it is important to save all ATM and debit receipts until they are reconciled with the bank statement. If there are any errors, they must be promptly reported to the bank. To be fully protected under the EFTA, in addition to reporting the loss or theft of a card, the customer must notify their financial institution of any errors, orally or in writing, no later than 60 days after the bank sends the bank statement containing the error.

It is preferable, however, to notify the bank by certified letter, return receipt requested, in order to prove that they received notice in a timely fashion. A copy of the letter and receipt should be kept in a safe place until the issue is resolved to the consumer's satisfaction.

USING THE ATM MACHINE

The ATM has been around since the mid-1960s. The first ATMs were strictly for getting cash using a bank-issued ATM card. Depending on the bank, in addition to dispensing cash, today's ATMs can accept deposits and loan payments, transfer funds between accounts, provide account information, including copies of canceled checks, and much more. Some ATMs even dispense postage stamps. When traveling in a foreign country, there will likely be an ATM somewhere that will be able to dispense cash using a debit or ATM card.

ATM Transaction Fees and Surcharges

ATMs are convenient, yet they can also be costly. For example, if you withdraw money from an ATM machine that is not owned by the bank that issued the card, the cardholder may incur a surcharge ranging from $1 to $4 per transaction. Federal law requires that an ATM alert a non-customer about a surcharge before a transaction is completed so the person can cancel the transaction if they wish.

To avoid unnecessary fees, it is best to try and use the issuing bank's own ATM whenever possible. Be aware that some banks also charge their own customers for ATM transactions, which may result in two charges—one from the ATM's owner, and the second from the card-issuing institution. In order to avoid surcharges altogether, the cardholder should request cash back when using a debit or ATM card to make purchases at a retail establishment, such as a supermarket, if that option is available.

Retained Card

On occasion, an ATM will not return the card to the customer following the transaction. Sometimes this is due to a defect in the card. This may also happen if the bank suspects fraudulent activity, e.g., if the customer repeatedly enters the wrong PIN number. If this should occur, immediately contact the financial institution that issued the card. They will issue a replacement card.

Error in Amount Dispensed

Sometimes an ATM malfunctions and does not dispense the amount of cash requested. If the receipt states that the amount of cash requested was dispensed, instead of the actual amount dispensed, immediately contact your bank to report the problem. The bank will check the machine to see if it has more money than it should have, in which case the difference will be refunded.

ATM Deposits

When making a deposit at an ATM, record the transaction in your checkbook, including information about each check that was deposited. Keep the ATM receipt and verify the deposit by reviewing your account statement, checking your account online, or by calling your bank's customer service line.

If you believe some or all of your deposit was mishandled, immediately contact your bank and follow up with a letter. If a check is missing, you might have to ask the check issuer to stop payment. Funds deposited in an ATM are not immediately available for withdrawal, and are subject to the bank's funds availability policy and federal schedules.

ATM Withdrawals

It is important to record all ATM withdrawals and purchases in the check register. Failure to enter the information and account for the withdrawals can cause unnecessary overdrafts due to bad recordkeeping. When using the ATM to check balances and transactions, do not rely on the balance reflected by the ATM machine. The ATM balance does not reflect deductions for checks written but not yet paid. The only way to know how much money is available is to accurately maintain one's checkbook.

Safety Considerations

ATM manufacturers and financial institutions try to make ATM use as safe as possible. They install sophisticated cameras, place ATMs in safe locations, provide adequate lighting, limit the maximum daily cash withdrawals, and employ other security measures. Nevertheless, thieves still target ATM users. In order to reduce the possibility of becoming a victim, the following safeguards should be followed:

1. Know where your ATM card is at all times, and do not keep your PIN number written down anywhere on or near the card. A thief who has both the ATM card and PIN number can quickly withdraw money from your account. If possible, memorize the PIN number, and do not share the number with anyone. Destroy old ATM cards, cutting through the account number and magnetic strip before throwing the card away.

2. Only visit ATMs that are in safe, well-lit areas, particularly at night. If anyone is loitering at or near the ATM, stay away. Look around for unusual looking devices on or near the ATM that may be used to record or intercept your PIN number.

3. Protect your ATM card when you use it to make purchases at retail establishments. For example, if you give an employee your card and you notice that he or she swipes it through two devices instead of one, that second device could be recording your account information for use in making a fraudulent card. Report any suspicious activity to the bank that issued the card.

4. Be careful when using private ATMs, such as those located in retail establishments. These ATMS are not owned by financial institutions but by non-banking companies and individuals. It is better to use an ATM at a FDIC-insured bank. If you must use a private ATM, only use ATMs at establishments you trust. Private ATMs have been known to be a source of fraudulent activity by dishonest owners who collect card numbers for use in making duplicate cards.

5. Withdraw the dispensed cash safely and immediately put the money in your wallet or pocket. Do not count the money at the machine. When using a bank's drive-up ATM, keep the engine running, the doors locked, and all of the windows rolled up after competing your transaction.

ONLINE BANKING

Online banking is relatively easy, even for the least computer savvy individual. Instead of standing on long lines, banking customers are now able to do most of their banking from home on their personal computer. For example, one can now view statements and transactions, open and close accounts, purchase investment products, apply for a mortgage, transfer funds among accounts, pay bills, and much more, right from their computer.

Online banking is a rapidly growing technology now available through most banks. The service is generally offered to the customer for free or at a small monthly charge. Studies have indicated that there is substantial customer demand for these services and banks may have to offer this service in order to stay competitive. However, fear of identity theft has deterred many from conducting their financial transactions online. This is because online banking customers must necessarily divulge a lot of their personal identifying and financial information in order to participate. To be safe, the consumer must make sure they are dealing with a legitimate institution, as set forth below.

Confirm that the Online Bank Is Legitimate

Whether you are dealing with a traditional bank or an online bank that has no physical offices, you must make sure that it is legitimate and that your deposits are federally insured. Read key information about the bank posted on its website. Most bank websites have an "About Us" section or something similar that describes the institution. You may find a brief history of the bank, the official name and address of the bank's headquarters, and information about its insurance coverage from the FDIC.

Be aware of copycat websites that deliberately use a name or website address very similar to, but not the same as, that of a real financial institution. The intent is to lure you into clicking onto their website to obtain personal information, such as your account number and password. Always check to see that you have typed the correct website address for your bank before conducting a transaction.

To verify an online bank's insurance status, look for the familiar FDIC logo or the words "Member FDIC" or "FDIC Insured" on the website. Also check the FDIC's online database of FDIC-insured institutions. A positive match will display the official name of the bank, the date it became insured, its insurance certificate number, the main office location for the bank, and its primary government regulator. If your bank does not appear on this list, contact the FDIC. Some bank websites provide links directly to the FDIC's website to assist you in identifying or verifying the FDIC insurance protection of their deposits. Not all banks operating on the internet are insured by the FDIC. Many banks that are not FDIC-insured are chartered overseas. If you choose to use a bank chartered overseas, it is important for you to know that the FDIC may not insure your deposits.

Registering for Online Banking

In order to sign up for online banking, the customer accesses their bank's website and follows the procedure for setting up the online banking account. After providing the account number and other identifying information, the customer is generally asked to choose a username and a password that they will use to access their existing accounts electronically.

Once registered, the customer can generally view their bank statements online, including recent activity, download their statements to their computer, and view imaged copies of individual items, without having to wait for their statements in the mail. In addition, most banks also offer the customer the ability to view the long-term activity on their account. The customer may also be able to link all of their bank accounts, transfer funds between accounts, open new accounts, apply for loans, order checks, make investments, and pay bills online.

Unfortunately, identity thieves who are able to obtain the consumer's username and password are also able to access this wealth of information and services. Thus, consumers should safeguard their online banking password very carefully. It is just as valuable as the PIN number assigned to the consumer's ATM card. Don't use a password that can easily be guessed by an identity thief. It is also wise to change your password from time to time to minimize the risk that your account will be accessed. In addition, if you get an email asking you to confirm your password, do not respond without calling the bank directly.

Given the extensive amount of personal identifying and financial information involved in online banking, there are serious concerns relating to security issues, thus banks are very careful in selecting and developing an appropriate software system with a secure online server to process their customer's banking transactions. Customers should inquire about the bank's online security procedures to make sure that their information is secure and the risk of interception by identity thieves is minimized.

Online Banking Services

Services vary depending on the particular bank. Some banks provide a full range of services online, such as obtaining statements and viewing transactions, opening and closing accounts, applying for mortgages, transferring funds among accounts, and bill payment. Other banks may provide fewer online services, e.g., limited to the ability to view statements and transactions. Some banks charge a nominal monthly fee while others offer the service for free. Banks generally provide consumers with a "tour" of the website to demonstrate how online banking works, and offer online customer service.

Many banks offer the customer the option of linking all of their bank accounts, such as their checking and savings accounts. This gives the customer the ability to transfer funds between accounts as needed. Many banks also offer the customer the opportunity to open new accounts and make investments online. Loan applications may also be completed online and submitted electronically. Customers can also order checks and place stop payments on-line. In addition, many bank websites contain a wealth of valuable information for the consumer, offer various tutorials of interest to the consumer, and provide links to other informative finance-related websites.

Online Bill Payment

Online bill payment is becoming increasingly popular with consumers. Many banks that offer online banking also provide their customers with the ability to pay their bills online using their bank account. The bank generally provides a list of payees, and the customer chooses the payees from that list. If a payee is not listed, the customer must type in the payee's name, address, telephone number and the customer's account number with the payee. This information is then stored and the customer need only enter the payment amount and date for the particular payee when it is time to pay that bill. The customer can thereafter track the status of bill payments online at any time.

Depending on the payee, the bill will be paid either electronically or by a paper check which is printed and mailed by the bank. An increasing number of companies are now equipped to accept direct electronic payments, which are transmitted instantaneously. Nevertheless, it is still advisable to schedule payments approximately 5 days in advance to make sure the payees receive timely payments and avoid late charges.

The customer can also request automatic bill payment for bills that are paid in the same amount and at the same time each month, such as an installment loan. The bank will automatically make those payments from the customer's account each month. The customer must be careful, however, to notate the monthly deduction in their checking or saving account ledger each month.

Electronic Bills

Many companies are now offering their customers the option of receiving electronic bills (e-bills) instead of mailing a paper bill. The e-bill is transmitted to the customer over the internet. It contains all of the same information as the paper bill, and offers the customer the opportunity to pay the bill online.

Maintaining Privacy and Security

Despite the convenience and expediency of online banking, security is still a concern and causes many consumers to be reluctant to bank over the internet. Concerned customers should inquire about the bank's online security procedures to make sure that their information is secure and the risk of interception by identity thieves is minimized. For more detailed information on internet privacy issues are discussed more fully in Chapter 7 (Protecting Your Identity) of this Almanac.

RESOLVING COMPLAINTS

If you have a complaint concerning your bank, there are a number of steps you can take to try and resolve the problem, as set forth below.

Contact Your Bank

The first step in trying to resolve a complaint is to contact your bank directly. If your bank is a small, local bank, you should schedule a personal meeting with the branch manager. Often a face-to-face meeting will go along way to resolving a problem unlike a telephone call or letter-writing, which can be frustrating.

Most large banks have a customer service department that handles problem resolution. Call that department to discuss your concerns and find out what procedures you must follow to resolve your complaint. Get the name of the person you spoke with, and their mailing address, so you can send a follow-up letter confirming what was stated in the conversation, e.g., whether a refund will be issued, etc. Written notification is often required by the consumer protection laws.

Contact the Primary Federal Regulator

If your attempts to resolve your complaint at the bank level are not successful, contact your bank's primary federal regulator. Following are the five Federal Regulators of Depository Institutions:

Federal Deposit Insurance Corporation (FDIC)

The Federal Deposit Insurance Corporation (FDIC) supervises state-chartered banks that are not members of the Federal Reserve System, and insures deposits at banks and savings associations. Contact information for the FDIC is as follows:

Federal Deposit Insurance Corporation (FDIC)
3501 N. Fairfax Drive
Arlington, VA 22226
Tel: 877-275-3342
E-mail: consumer@fdic.gov
Website: www.fdic.gov

Office of the Comptroller of the Currency

The Office of the Comptroller of the Currency charters and supervises national banks. The word "National" appears in the name of a national bank, or the initials "N. A." follow its name. Contact information for the Office of the Comptroller of the Currency is as follows:

Office of the Comptroller of the Currency
Customer Assistance Unit
1301 McKinney Street, Suite 3450
Houston, TX 77010
Tel: 800-613-6743
E-mail: consumer.assistance@occ.treas.gov
Website: www.occ.treas.gov

Federal Reserve Board

The Federal Reserve Board supervises state-chartered banks that are members of the Federal Reserve System. Contact information for the Federal Reserve Board is as follows:

Federal Reserve Board
Division of Consumer and Community Affairs
Mail Stop 801
Washington, DC 20551
Tel: 202-452-3693
Website: www.federalreserve.gov

National Credit Union Administration

The National Credit Union Administration charters and supervises federal credit unions, and insures deposits at federal credit unions and many state credit unions. Contact information for the National Credit Union Administration is as follows:

National Credit Union Administration
1775 Duke Street
Alexandria, VA 22314-3428
Tel: 703-518-6300
E-mail: pacamail@ncua.gov
Website: www.ncua.gov

Office of Thrift Supervision

The Office of Thrift Supervision supervises federally and state-chartered savings associations, including federally chartered savings banks. The names generally identify them as savings and loan associations, savings associations or savings banks. Federally chartered savings associations have the word "Federal" or the initials "FSB" or "FA" in their names. Contact information for the Office of Thrift Supervision is as follows:

Office of Thrift Supervision
Consumer Affairs Office
1700 G Street, NW
Washington, DC 20552
Tel: 202-906-6000
E-mail: consumer.complaint@ots.treas.gov
Website: www.ots.treas.gov

If you are unsure about which Federal Regulator governs your financial institution, you can call the bank directly for this information, or obtain this information from the FDIC.

Filing a Complaint

The consumer does not have to know the law in order to file a complaint with a government agency. The agency is obligated to advise the consumer of his or her rights under the law, and whether those rights have been violated based on the facts presented.

When writing a complaint letter to a government agency, make sure to include the following information: (1) your name, address and telephone number; (2) the name and location of the institution; (3) a brief description of the problem and your efforts to resolve the problem, including the names of employees you contacted; and (4) the action you would like the institution to take to correct the problem. Attach copies of any supporting documents, such as letters, statements, etc.

The complaint letter should be signed by the person making the complaint. This authorizes the government agency to contact the institution on their behalf, and lets the institution know that the customer wants their information released.

CHAPTER 5:
AUTOMOBILES

BUYING AN AUTOMOBILE

Aside from one's home, an automobile is generally the second largest purchase a consumer makes. Buying an automobile is a very important transaction that must be considered carefully if one does not want to risk a costly mistake. Following are points to consider involving the purchase of your automobile.

New Automobile Purchases

A new car is a large-ticket item which must be thoroughly researched before purchasing. Don't rush into a new car purchase before checking with consumer publications concerning the vehicle's ratings for safety, quality, and cost comparison, etc. Make sure you carefully read every document you are asked to sign. Most new cars come with some kind of warranty. Make sure you carefully read your warranty and know what is covered and what is not covered. If you don't understand certain terms, get professional advice. Don't rely on the salesperson's representations. The salesperson's primary interest is to sell you the car. Don't be pressured into making a deal you will regret with costly consequences later.

Keep copies of the documents about your car, including warranties, advertisements, and brochures in case the car fails to conform. Inspect your new car before you accept delivery. If you detect any problems, refuse delivery until the problem has been fixed. Don't accept delivery and hope the problem can be fixed later.

Used Automobile Purchases

Before shopping for a used vehicle, you should check out used car guides, newspaper ads and classifieds to get an idea of a fair price range for the particular car you are seeking. Contact the Auto Safety

Hotline at (800) 424-9393 for recall information on the type of car you intend to purchase.

Before purchasing the car, make sure you take a test drive. Bring your own mechanic with you so he or she can inspect the vehicle. You are entitled to information concerning previous ownership of the car, including its mechanical history, and whether it has been involved in any accidents. Obtain the car's vehicle identification number (VIN) so you can obtain an independent vehicle history report.

Make sure that you carefully read the purchase agreement prior to signing to ensure that it accurately reflects the details of the transaction. If you were promised something that is not written in the agreement, make sure that it is included before you sign. Inquire about the warranty provisions of the car and make sure you get them in writing. Used cars may still be under the manufacturer's original warranty, or you may be able to purchase an extended warranty. Make sure you carefully read your warranty and know what is covered and what is not covered. Also, ask to see the maintenance and service records for the car, if available.

Some unscrupulous used car dealers fail to register the car in the dealer name to avoid being subject to the law. Instead, they maintain the registration in the previous owner's name and make the deal as if you were buying the car from the private individual. Make sure you check the vehicle registration and title to ensure that the seller is the registered owner of the vehicle.

Vehicle Title Washing

Vehicle title washing refers to vehicles that have been severely damaged in one state, and then rebuilt and sold in another state where a new title is obtained and the purchaser has no idea that the car was once a wreck. These cars are likely to break down and cause the unwary purchaser a lot of repair costs not to mention the safety concerns.

A minority of states, including California, Michigan, and Iowa, have consumer protection laws that prohibit the retitling of a vehicle that has been totaled and is unrepairable. Many states do not have such protection, and vehicles are often moved into those states, retitled and sold to unsuspecting buyers.

There is federal legislation pending that would provide a uniform national standard for handling wrecked and salvaged vehicles, and that would require warning labels on rebuilt salvage cars—e.g., cars that sustained damage exceeding a certain percentage of the car's pre-accident value. The law would also require owners of wrecked and salvaged vehicles to disclose any damage exceeding a certain dollar amount.

It may be difficult to spot a car that has been title washed. If the car has an out-of-state title, check to see if the title indicates whether the car has been salvaged. If not, you can try and inspect the car to see whether it has had any damage, e.g., mismatched paint; misaligned hood or trunk, etc. Have a mechanic inspect the underbody of the vehicle to see whether the frame has been bent. Check for rust in the interior that may indicate water damage.

LEASING AN AUTOMOBILE

An automobile lease is a contract between the owner of the automobile (the "lessor") and the party who leases the automobile for his or her own use (the "lessee"), subject to the terms and limitations contained in the contract, for a specific period of time, and at a specific payment. Thus, the parties to the automobile lease are known as the lessor and the lessee. Usually, the original lessor is a dealership or an independent leasing company.

A consumer lease is a lease between the lessor and lessee for the use of personal property, that is used primarily for personal, family, or household purposes, for a period of more than 4 months, with a total contractual obligation of no more than $25,000. If the lease meets all of the foregoing requirements, it is governed by the Consumer Leasing Act and the Federal Reserve Board's Regulation M. If the lease does not meet all of these requirements— e.g., the leased property is used primarily for business and not personal purposes—the Consumer Leasing Act and Regulation M do not apply.

Read the Leasing Agreement Carefully

Read the leasing agreement carefully before signing to make sure all of the terms you negotiated are in writing. If it is not in writing, it is generally not enforceable. Important items to review are as follows:

1. If you negotiated the value of the vehicle, make sure the negotiated amount appears in the "agreed-upon value of the vehicle" line on the lease form.

2. If you have a trade-in, make sure the negotiated net value appears on the "net trade-in allowance" line on the lease form.

3. If you make a cash payment for the "amount due at lease signing or delivery" for the first payment, security deposit, and/or capitalized cost reduction, make sure this amount appears on the "amount to be paid in cash" line on the lease form.

4. If a rebate or discount is included in the deal, make sure this amount has been credited in the "amount due at lease signing or delivery" on the lease form.

You must make sure there are no spaces left blank in the document. If the item does not apply, either cross it our or write "N/A" in the blank space.

Make sure you understand all of the terms and conditions. If you are not sure, ask questions. Once you sign the lease agreement, both you and the lessor are obligated to abide by all of the lease terms.

The lessor is legally required to provide you with a copy of your federal lease disclosures. State laws determine whether you are entitled to copies of all the other documents that you sign. Nevertheless, you should request copies of all documents that you sign. The lease must be signed by you and the lessor in order to be binding.

Lease Cancellation

Generally, you do not have an automatic cancellation period after signing the lease agreement. However, if the lease agreement was signed at your home or business instead of the lessor's office, you may have a 3-day right to cancellation under federal law. State law may provide additional cancellation rights; therefore, the reader is advised to check the law of his or her jurisdiction. In addition, some lessors provide for a cancellation period in the leasing agreement.

The Federal Consumer Leasing Act – Regulation M

In 1976, the Truth in Lending Act was amended to include the Federal Consumer Leasing Act. Under the Federal Consumer Leasing Act – Regulation M, a vehicle lessor must provide the consumer with certain information before the automobile lease agreement is signed. The required disclosures must be written clearly and conspicuously, and must be given to the consumer in a dated statement prior to the lease signing.

State Leasing Laws

Some state laws may provide you with additional rights related to automobile leasing. However, a state law that is inconsistent with the provisions of the Federal Consumer Leasing Act and Regulation M is preempted to the extent of the inconsistency, unless the state law gives greater protection and benefit to the consumer.

Default and Respossession

When you lease an automobile, the lease agreement gives the lessor certain rights and remedies against you in case you default on any of the provisions of the lease agreement. Therefore, it is important that you read your lease carefully to determine what acts constitute a default of the lease agreement.

If you anticipate that you will be unable to comply with any of the provisions of the lease agreement, e.g., you do not have the money for the monthly lease payment, you should contact the lessor to try and work out a solution instead of waiting for the lessor to seize your automobile. It is much easier to prevent the seizure from happening in the first place than to deal with the aftermath of repossession. In many cases, a lessor will work out a revised payment plan.

Nevertheless, the lease agreement does give the lessor the right to repossess the automobile if they choose to do so, and they may refuse to work out a repayment plan, or overlook a default of any of the lease agreement provisions. If the lessor takes such a strict stance, you may be able to avoid some of the costs of repossession by voluntarily agreeing to surrender the automobile. However, even if you voluntarily surrender the automobile, you will still be responsible for paying any amounts owed, including deficiency amounts, early termination fees, and other related costs.

In most states, the lessor can legally repossess your automobile if you are in default on the lease agreement, without having to obtain a court order, and without giving you advance notice of the repossession. Some states even allow the lessor to enter upon your property to seize the automobile. Some states have certain procedures the lessor must follow before he or she can repossess your vehicle, and if the lessor violates those procedures, they may have to pay you damages. Thus, the reader is advised to check the law of his or her jurisdiction in this regard.

Even if state law permits the lessor to seize your vehicle, the law usually prohibits the lessor from committing a "breach of peace" when carrying out the repossession. For example, some states consider seizing an automobile from a closed garage a "breach of peace," in which case the lessor may be liable to you for any damage done to your property during the seizure.

Once the lessor seizes your automobile, they generally have the right to either keep it, or sell it in a public or private sale or auction. Depending on state law, the lessor may be required to notify you as to the course of action they intend to take, e.g., advise you of the time and place the vehicle will be auctioned.

If the lessor chooses to sell the automobile, the sale must be conducted in a commercially reasonable manner—i.e., according to the standards and customs of the marketplace. For example, the lessor cannot price the vehicle at the highest possible price, nor can the lessor sell the automobile for a price far below fair market value. Depending on state law, if the lessor fails to sell the automobile in a commercially reasonable manner, you may be able to sue the lessor for damages.

If your automobile is seized, the lessor is not permitted to keep or sell any personal property left in the vehicle. If personal items are missing from your automobile, you may be entitled to compensation for the loss.

Reinstatement of the Lease Agreement

Some states allow you to reinstate your lease agreement for the seized automobile provided you cure the breach—e.g., pay any outstanding monthly payments due on the lease—and pay all of the costs of repossession, including legal fees. However, if you subsequently cause another default of the lease agreement, your automobile can once again be repossessed and sold.

AUTOMOBILE LEMON LAWS

A "lemon" is a term used to describe a car with a chronic defect that substantially impairs the car's use, value or safety. The key term is "substantial impairment." If the paint has started to peel prematurely, or the radio volume control doesn't work properly, your car will not qualify as a "lemon." However, if the brakes continually fail, or the car doesn't steer properly, after you have tried to have the problem repaired, you likely bought a lemon.

All 50 states and the District of Columbia have enacted laws that protect consumers who have purchased a car that turns out to be a "lemon." A lemon law generally entitles the consumers to a replacement vehicle or a refund for a chronically defective car that the manufacturer has been unable to fix despite a reasonable number of repair attempts.

Lemon laws do not cover defects that result from an accident, neglect, or abuse. In addition, there is no coverage for defects that arise from modification or alteration of the car by persons other than the manufacturer or its authorized service agent.

Many state lemon laws are tied in with the particular state's inspection requirement. Depending on the state, safety inspections may cover a number of items on a car, including the brakes, tires, seatbelts, lights, etc. If the car fails this safety inspection within a certain time period after the purchase, and the cost of repair exceeds the state's set amount, which is often computed as a percentage of the purchase price, the consumer may be able to recover under the state's lemon law.

Due to variations in state lemon law requirements, the reader is advised to check their own state's lemon law statute for specific provisions.

A directory of state lemon law websites is set forth in Appendix 14.

In addition, your state attorney general's office, consumer protection agency, and state lemon law contacts can also provide you with copies of your state's lemon law.

Covered Vehicles

All state lemon laws cover new cars provided the car is purchased for personal, family or household use. About half of the states have a lemon law that covers leased cars, but only Arizona, Connecticut, Hawaii, Maine, Massachusetts, Minnesota, New Jersey, New York and Rhode Island have lemon laws that cover used cars. However, if your car is a "Certified Used Vehicle"—i.e., it came with a manufacturer warranty— it is generally considered a "new" car and thus covered under the lemon law.

The Lemon Law Presumption

Some states, such as California, have a "lemon law presumption." Under this presumption, any defect or condition that substantially impairs the use, value or safety of your vehicle under warranty, that you have tried to have repaired by an authorized dealer, entitles you to seek a refund or replacement under the state's lemon law, even if the manufacturer continues to say it cannot find a problem. The legal presumption recognizes that if you purchased a new car, you have the right to rely on its dependability and safety.

Legislation

In addition to state lemon laws, those engaged in the business of selling automobiles are subject to numerous additional state and federal laws, such as the federal Magnuson-Moss Warranty Act, the federal Odometer Act, and Article 2 of the Uniform Commercial Code, which covers contracts dealing with the sale of defective products.

Most state lemon laws are based upon the federal Magnuson-Moss Warranty Act, which makes breach of warranty a violation of federal law. The Act gives consumers considerable rights in dealing with manufacturers and car-dealers of lemon automobiles. This law guarantees a car buyer that certain minimum requirements of warranties must be met, and provides for disclosure of warranties before purchase. Under the Act, if the product—the lemon car—has a written warranty, and if any part of the product—or the product itself—is considered defective, the warrantor must permit the buyer the choice of either a refund or replacement of the product. The Act also provides that the consumer may sue the manufacturer to enforce his or her rights.

A consumer may also find a remedy within their state's warranty laws and consumer protection statute prohibiting unfair and deceptive acts and practices. If you have a defective car that is not covered under your state's lemon law, you may still have recourse under these laws. Therefore, the reader is advised to check the law of his or her own jurisdiction for additional protection.

Preparing a Lemon Law Claim

If you want to prevail on your lemon law claim, it is crucial that you prepare carefully. You are up against manufacturers and dealerships that pose a strong opposition. You must keep detailed records, and follow the prescribed procedures required by the law. Depending on the particular state, this may include (1) providing proper notice of the defect and giving the manufacturer a reasonable opportunity to repair the car; (2) asking the manufacturer to give you a replacement car or refund; and, if the manufacturer refuses, (3) utilizing lemon law arbitration programs before going to court. In any event, your success depends in large part on the documentation you provide in support of your claim.

You must provide evidence in order to prevail in your lemon law claim. Gather all of the information and documentation that proves your claim. Types of information and documentation that will help support your claim include repair orders and invoices. In addition, you should keep a vehicle repair log in order to adequately demonstrate the number of times you had to take your car in to be repaired, and the details of the repair attempt. This way, when you approach your manufacture for a replacement car or refund, it will be easy to explain the problems you have been having, as well as your consistent but unsuccessful efforts to get the condition repaired.

The Repair Log

The repair log is a detailed summary of the attempted repairs performed on your car. Your repair log should show the dates, mileage, and complaints for every visit you've made to the dealer to have your vehicle repaired. Your repair log should note whether or not the defect could be repaired.

Following is information which should be included in your repair log.

1. Vehicle information, such as make, model, license plate number, vehicle identification number, etc.

2. The date you purchased your vehicle.

3. The odometer reading as of the date you took possession of your car.

4. The dates and actual mileage for each time you took your vehicle in for repair.

5. The repair completion dates and actual mileage for each time you picked up your vehicle.

6. The name of the dealer or authorized repair shop where your vehicle is taken.

7. The repair order number printed on the repair work order.

8. A description of the work requested or a detailed description of the problem that needs to be repaired. Again, each time you bring your car in for the same problem, you must make sure you describe the problem identically on the work order. Don't leave it up to the service technician to describe the problem.

9. A description of the actual work performed as shown on the invoice you receive when you pick up your car. If the dealer refuses to give you an invoice—e.g., because the vehicle was under warranty and there was no charge—make a note of the dealer's refusal in your repair log.

10. The cost of repairs, including incidental charges such as towing or car rental. Attach copies of all receipts.

If the problem or defect is not corrected, note that in your repair log and bring the car back to the dealer for another repair attempt. Make sure you note the details of the new repair attempt in your repair log.

Keep Notes of Conversations

You should write down the names of all persons you speak with about the problem or defect, including the mechanic who works on the car, customer service representatives, service department personnel, etc. Note the date, time and the specifics of what was discussed during each conversation. Your complaints should always be made in writing, and you should keep a copy of your complaint in your file.

Technical Service Bulletins

Technical Service Bulletins are alerts sent from the manufacturer to the dealership concerning defects found in certain car models. The bulletins advise dealers of repairs that should be made on the affected cars. Although these bulletins are not made public, you can obtain copies of any bulletins released for your particular make and model car from the dealer. The National Highway and Traffic Safety Administration (NHTSA) also maintains a list of bulletins. Contact information for the NHTSA is:

National Highway and Traffic Safety Administration
Telephone: 800-424-9393
Website: www.nhtsa.dot.gov.

Maintenance Records

In order to support your claim under your state's lemon law, you will need to show that you properly maintained your car according to the manufacturer's recommendations. Otherwise, a claim may be made that the car's problems were caused by your negligence instead of a manufacturing defect. Routine maintenance includes oil changes, engine tune-ups, checking fluids, rotating tires, etc.

Your Remedies Under State Lemon Laws

State lemon laws generally entitle the consumer to a replacement car or a refund if the car they purchased is unable to be repaired. You may also be able to recover the costs associated with the purchase, such as registration and titling fees, finance charges, sales tax, etc. You should also request reimbursement for any repair costs. However, if you continue to drive the car while your claim is pending, the law may permit the seller to deduct a certain amount from any refund you are awarded based on the mileage you put on the car.

Lemon Law Arbitration

If the manufacturer refuses to give you a replacement car or a refund, you can try using the manufacturer's in-house arbitration procedure, if there is one in place. Various auto manufacturers and dealers have established their own arbitration programs. In some states, the law requires you to participate in any state-certified in-house arbitration proceeding before you are permitted to sue in court, provided the in-house proceeding complies with the state's lemon law and the federal regulations. "State-certified" generally means that the manufacturer's arbitration procedure meets certain state and federal requirements; however, it does not mean that the program is administered or sponsored by the state.

Arbitration is state-run in Connecticut, Florida, Georgia, Hawaii, Maine, Massachusetts, New Hampshire, New Jersey, New York, Texas, Vermont and Washington. In other states, arbitration programs are run by the manufacturer, the Better Business Bureau or the National Automobile Dealers Association.

If you are permitted to choose your own arbitrator, it is advisable to use a Better Business Bureau arbitration program or a state consumer protection arbitration program instead of the manufacturer's in-house program.

Going To Court

If there is no state-certified arbitration program, or if the state's law gives you the right to go directly to court, you can file a lawsuit against the manufacturer. You can also go to court if you are dissatisfied with the arbitrator's decision, provided the decision was not binding. If you go to court, you should hire an attorney to assist you, as litigation is more formal and more complex than arbitration. The attorney should be experienced with the state's lemon law and consumer warranty law, and should be one who routinely represents consumers and not automobile manufacturers. If you prevail in court, you may be able to recover a greater refund, including costs and attorney fees.

AUTOMOBILE RENTAL

The cost of renting an automobile varies greatly among different rental agencies. Before renting a car, check the rates of several agencies to get the best deal for your particular situation. Some agencies charge a low rental fee but recoup the difference in mileage charges. Others may charge a higher rental fee but offer unlimited mileage. The rates may also differ depending on the location where you pick up the car, e.g. an urban branch may be more expensive than an airport pick-up, or vice-versa.

Before you leave the parking area, carefully inspect the car for damage, however slight. If there are scratches or dents, write them down and give them to the rental agent for their file. Most agencies hold the consumer liable for any damage to the vehicle. Of course, they generally offer optional insurance coverage, however, it can add a significant cost to your total rental charges. Check with your credit card company or your own car insurance agent to see whether there is any coverage available. If you are covered privately, you can save on your rental charges and avoid duplicating coverage.

Presently, there are no federal laws which pertain to short-term car rentals. Automobile rental may be governed by state law. The reader is advised to check the law of his or her own jurisdiction.

AUTOMOBILE REPAIRS

Automobile repair shops are notorious for overcharging their customers or for charging customers for work which either was not done, or wasn't needed. Seek a referral from friends or relatives who are satisfied with their repair shop. If you are unsure about a particular shop, check them out with your local state or consumer protection office or local Better Business Bureau to see if any complaints have been filed.

It would be wise to get several written estimates before choosing the shop to do the work. Make sure that work is not done until and unless authorized by you in writing. Never sign a blank work order. Inquire about the warranty available on the repair being done and ask that it be reduced to writing. Ask the shop to return the old parts to you so you can compare replaced items with the work order. Make sure you keep copies of all paperwork for your files.

CHAPTER 6:
PRIVACY RIGHTS AND THE INTERNET

MAINTAINING YOUR PRIVACY ON THE INTERNET

Although the Internet is a revolutionary tool for marketing, banking and communication, it has unfortunately spawned a whole new venue for identity thieves. The Internet enhances the availability and accessibility of personal identifying information, and thus creates greater risks for consumers and greater opportunities for criminal activity, including identity theft.

For example, consumers now use the Internet to handle their banking and make online purchases using credit cards and debit cards. Signing up for services generally requires the consumer to provide personal information, including financial information, in order to register. Identity thieves are constantly seeking to decode the massive amount of data being transmitted on the Internet.

In addition, there are many scams being perpetrated on the Internet which fool the consumer into revealing personal information. A fraud complaint is "Internet-related" if: (1) it concerns an Internet product or service; (2) the company initially contacts the consumer via the Internet; or (3) the consumer responds via the Internet.

According to the Federal Trade Commission (FTC), in 2005, there were 196,503 internet-related fraud complaints filed. Therefore, it is critical that Internet users become familiar with the most common Internet schemes and carefully safeguard their personal information to minimize the risk of being an identity theft victim.

The following precautions should be taken in order to avoid online fraud and the interception of personal information:

1. Patronize websites of reputable, familiar companies, such as companies who also operate retail stores or mail order catalogues.

---

2. Patronize companies that display a privacy seal on their website, and read the website's privacy statement to determine their privacy practices.

3. Make sure the company has a physical address and a telephone number so that they can be contacted off-line. A company that lists a post office box instead of a physical address, or one that discloses no contact information, may be a fly-by-night operation set up for illegal purposes.

4. Check with the state Attorney General's Office to see whether there are any adverse reports about the particular company.

5. Give out only the amount of information that is necessary for you to complete the online transaction.

6. When dealing with an unfamiliar company, start out by purchasing a small, inexpensive item to determine how the company handles the order.

7. Use a unique password when registering on a site, randomly combining letters and numbers, and never disclose the password to anyone.

8. Do not send private information by email.

9. Check to make sure you are actually on the official website of the company you want to patronize. Criminals have been known to create websites with names similar to legitimate businesses in order to intercept personal information. One way of checking the legitimacy of a website is to visit http://www.whois.net, a service which sets forth the identity of the registrant of the URL, and the physical address of the company.

10. Often companies hold contests in order to collect names and contact information for future marketing. When deciding whether to enter a contest, consider whether you want the company operating the contest to have access to your personal information.

WEBSITE PRIVACY POLICIES

It is important to check the privacy policy for any website you visit and find out whether the company sells or shares its visitors' identifying information before submitting your personal information. If the privacy policy indicates that the company does compile such information, it is best not to visit that website or you risk opening yourself up to more unsolicited commercial email. Some websites allow the user to "opt out" of receiving email from third parties if the user so chooses.

When visiting a website, it is important to check whether the website has a privacy statement, particularly if the website requests the user to enter personal information. A privacy statement describes the way in which the website collects, shares and protects the user's personal information. It is a legally binding document which the website owner must abide by or face legal action.

Internet users should carefully read the privacy policy of all websites with which they do business, including the privacy policy of their own internet service provider. Any website that asks for personal information should have a privacy policy statement. If a website does not post a privacy statement, the user is advised not to patronize that website.

Elements of a Privacy Statement

A website's privacy statement should be easily accessible and understandable. Some websites post a simplified version of their privacy policy that is easy for users to read, and provide links to additional information, which may contain more complicated legal or technical information.

A well-drafted privacy policy should provide the user with the following information:

1. The information that is being collected.

2. Whether the information is personally identifiable.

3. The reasons the website collects the information.

4. The appropriateness of the data collection as it relates to the particular activity or transaction.

5. The manner in which the data is collected.

6. Whether the user has a choice regarding the type and quantity of personal information that the site collects.

7. Whether the website uses cookies.

8. Whether the website maintains web logs.

9. How the personal information collected is used by the website.

10. Whether personal information is ever used for a secondary purpose—i.e., a purpose other than that for which the user has provided the information.

11. If personal information is used for a secondary purpose, the user should be so informed.

12. Whether the visitor has consented to secondary use of personal information.

13. Whether the visitor has the option to prohibit secondary use of personal information.

14. Whether the website offers different kinds of service depending on user privacy preferences, e.g., does the website disadvantage users who exercise data collection choices.

15. Whether the user can access the information collected.

16. Whether the user can correct inaccurate data that has been collected.

17. The length of time personal information is stored.

18. The website's complaint procedures.

19. Contact information, such as an e-mail address or phone number, so the user can contact the company if they have any questions about online security or their privacy policy statement..

20. The laws governing data collection.

21. Whether the website collecting the information is regulated by the Privacy Act or any other privacy law.

A sample privacy policy outline is set forth at Appendix 15 of this Almanac.

PRIVACY SEAL PROGRAMS

Privacy seals are branded symbols of trust on the Internet similar to the Good Housekeeping "seal of approval." They give added assurance that a website is abiding by its posted privacy statement.

Privacy seal programs offer third-party verification and monitoring of the information practices of websites. These programs have also established complaint and resolution procedures for users who believe that their privacy has been violated by a program participant.

The TRUSTe Privacy Seal Program

TRUSTe is an independent, non-profit initiative working to build consumer trust and confidence on the Internet. TRUSTe is responsible for developing the first online privacy seal program. The TRUSTe privacy seal program assures consumers that the websites they visit are compliant with fair information practices approved by the U.S. Department of Commerce, the Federal Trade Commission and prominent industry-represented organizations and associations.

Participant Verification

A website that is a member of the TRUSTe seal program will display a TRUSTe privacy seal on the website's privacy statement. When the user clicks on the privacy seal, they will be directed to a validation page on the TRUSTe website. If the user is not directed to the validation page, the user should be aware that the website may be displaying a fraudulent TRUSTe seal.

To verify that the website is a member of the TRUSTe seal program, consumers can view a list of participants on the TRUSTe website at: (www.truste.org/ about/member_list.php)

Filing a Privacy Violation Complaint

If a user believes that a TRUSTe participant has committed a privacy violation, an online complaint—referred to as a "watchdog"—should be filed with TRUSTe at: (www.truste.org/consumers/watchdog_service.php)

TRUSTe will investigate the complaint and confirm that the website is a TRUSTe participant. TRUSTe can only act on privacy violation complaints, and can only accept complaints about a company that is a participant in the program. TRUSTe will then contact the website and make inquiries about the complaint. TRUSTe may also contact the user to get more information about their complaint. TRUSTe will contact the participating company and respond to the user within 10 business days. The participating company has 5 days after that to respond to TRUSTe and the user.

Depending on the nature of the complaint, TRUSTe may require the participating company to change its stated privacy policy or privacy practices. TRUSTe will also have the user's information corrected, modified, or deleted, as appropriate. A company that refuses to comply with a TRUSTe decision may be referred to the appropriate government agency, removed from the TRUSTe program, and be subject to legal action with TRUSTe. Either party to the complaint may file an appeal of a TRUSTe decision within 10 days of receipt of the decision.

The BBBOnline Privacy Seal Program

BBBOnline is a wholly owned subsidiary of the Council of Better Business Bureaus. BBBOnline also operates a privacy seal program which requires its website participants to exercise responsible privacy practices.

Participant Verification

A website that is a BBBOnline participant will display a privacy seal on the website's homepage or on its privacy statement. The seal provides a link to the validation page of the BBBOnline website.

To verify that the website is a member of the BBBOnline seal program, consumers can view a list of participants on the BBBOnline website at: (www.bbbonline.org/consumer/Privindex.aspx)

Filing a Privacy Violation Complaint

If a user believes that a BBBOnline participant has committed a privacy violation, an online complaint—referred to as a "watchdog"—should be filed with TRUSTe at: (www.bbbonline.org/consumer/complaint.asp)

BBBOnline will review the complaint. Users are asked to include the following items with their complaint:

1. A copy of all correspondence between the user and the organization or company that operates the website.

2. Information for identification purposes.

3. Information about which included materials are confidential and which are not.

BBBOnline will determine the eligibility of the complaint, and evaluate, investigate, analyze, and make a decision about how to resolve the complaint. The complaint will be forwarded to the website for its comments, and will also contact the both parties if it needs additional information.

The website has 15 business days to respond to the complaint. Once the answer is received, it is forwarded to the user, who has 10 days to submit any additional information. The reply is then forwarded to the website, which has an additional 10 days to reply. After all information is submitted, a decision will be rendered.

Depending on the nature of the complaint, BBBOnline may require the participating company to change its stated privacy policy or privacy practices. BBBOnline will also have the user's information corrected, modified, or deleted, as appropriate. A company that refuses to comply with a BBBOnline decision may be referred to the appropriate government agency, removed from the BBBOnline program, and be subject to legal action with BBBOnline.

BBBOnLine also provides an appeals process for matters involving substantial questions or interpretations of BBBOnLine privacy standards, or in situations in which there is a significant possibility that the matter might be decided differently.

THE CHILDREN'S ONLINE PRIVACY PROTECTION ACT (COPPA)

The Children's Online Privacy Protection Act (COPPA) and the FTC's implementing Rule took effect April 21, 2000. The primary goal of the Act and the Rule is to place parents in control over what information is collected from their children online. The COPPA Rule applies to operators of commercial websites and online services directed to children under 13 that collect personal information from children, and operators of general audience sites with actual knowledge that they are collecting information from children under 13.

The COPPA Rule requires the website operator to post a link to a notice of its information practices on the home page of its website or online service and at each area where it collects personal information from children. The link to the privacy notice must be clearly written, understandable and prominent. It must state the following information: (1) the name and contact information, including address, telephone number and email address, of all operators collecting or maintaining children's personal information through the website or online service; (2) the kinds of personal information collected from children and how the information is collected—e.g., directly from the child, or passively through cookies; (3) how the operator uses the personal information; (4) whether the operator discloses information collected from children to third parties; (5) that the parent has the option to agree to the collection and use of the child's information without consenting to the disclosure of the information to third parties; (6) that the operator may not require a child to disclose more information than is reasonably necessary to participate in an activity as a condition of participation; and (7) that the parent can review the child's personal information, ask to have it deleted and refuse to allow any further collection or use of the child's information.

Before collecting, using or disclosing personal information from a child, an operator must obtain verifiable parental consent from the child's parent. The regulations include several exceptions that allow operators to collect a child's email address without getting the parent's consent in advance. These exceptions cover many popular online activities for kids, including contests, online newsletters, homework help and electronic postcards.

Operators must use reasonable procedures to ensure they are dealing with the child's parent before they provide access to the child's specific information. They can use a variety of methods to verify the parent's identity, including: (1) obtaining a signed form from the parent via regular mail or fax; (2) accepting and verifying a credit card number; (3) taking calls from parents on a toll-free telephone number staffed by trained personnel; (4) email accompanied by digital signature; and (5) email accompanied by a PIN or password obtained through one of the verification methods above.

Operators who follow one of these procedures acting in good faith to a request for parental access are protected from liability under federal and state law for inadvertent disclosures of a child's information to someone who purports to be a parent.

The FTC monitors the Internet for compliance with the Rule and brings law enforcement actions where appropriate to deter violations. Parents and other concerned individuals can submit complaints to the FTC for investigation. The FTC may impose civil penalties for violations of the Rule in the same manner as for other Rules under the FTC Act. For more information, the FTC has set up a special web page designed for children, parents, businesses, and educators (http://www.ftc.gov/kidzprivacy/).

MAKE SURE YOUR ONLINE TRANSACTIONS ARE SECURE

Although it may be impossible to protect oneself completely from fraud and deception when making online purchases, there are some steps the consumer can take to make it less likely they will be an identity theft victim. The consumer is advised to make sure that their online purchases are made using a secure browser to protect the consumer's personal information against fraud.

A secure browser refers to software that encrypts or scrambles the purchase information sent over the Internet. The consumer should be sure that the browser they use has the latest encryption capabilities available and should comply with industry security standards. Most computers come with a browser installed. Some browsers are available for downloading over the Internet at no cost to the consumer.

In addition to making sure you use a secure browser before providing personal identifying or financial information on a particular website, it is important to review the site's privacy policy to ascertain the security features offered by the site. Do not divulge any private information if you are not satisfied that the website is secure.

One way of knowing whether or not a website is using a security system is to watch the address bar on the screen. At the point where the consumer enters their personal information, the prefix on the address should change to "shttp" or "https." Scroll left to determine whether the prefix changed. If you are unsure, contact the business directly to find out about their online security system and privacy policy.

If the website states that your personal identifying or financial information does not need to be encrypted, do not patronize the website. In addition, if the company does not have a physical address, and you are unfamiliar with it, do not conduct online business with the company, as it may be a fly-by-night operation set up for illegal purposes.

Following your online purchase, the website usually generates a receipt that can be printed. The consumer should print out and retain this information and any other order confirmation sent by the merchant to the consumer's email address. This information should be checked against the consumer's monthly credit card and bank statements. If there are any discrepancies, errors, or unauthorized purchases, the credit card issuer or bank should be notified immediately.

USE YOUR EMAIL SYSTEM CAREFULLY

Internet users communicate with each other online using email and instant messages. All kinds of information can be sent via email, including text messages, letters, documents, pictures, etc. It is an immediate way of transmitting information to others, and has become very popular as a means of communication in both personal and business affairs. Unfortunately, communicating online does not afford the same level of privacy that written correspondence offers. Following are some tips for making sure your email is secure and your personal information is kept confidential.

Encryption

Email is generally not secure and can be intercepted and read by others. Therefore, it would be unwise to transmit any personal identifying or financial information by email unless you use email cryptography software to scramble your messages in code. Encryption is a method of scrambling an email message or file so that it is gibberish to anyone who does not know how to unscramble it. The privacy advantage of encryption is that anything encrypted is virtually inaccessible to anyone other than the designated recipient. Thus, private information may be encrypted and then transmitted, stored, or distributed without fear that it will be read by others.

Use An Anonymous Remailer

Anonymous remailers were created to address privacy risks and concerns by allowing the user to send anonymous email messages. An anonymous remailer is a special email server that acts as a middleman and strips outgoing email of all personally identifying information, then forwards it to its destination, usually with the IP address of the remailer attached.

Delete Stored Email

Every time an email message is sent, a number of copies of that email message are created. One copy is stored locally on the sender's computer, another on the sender's ISP system, another on the recipient's computer, and one copy is stored on the recipient's ISP system. You can delete the stored copy of your email by opening the "sent mail" folder in the email program and delete the email by removing it to the trash folder, and then emptying the trash folder.

Limit Email Forwarding

Recipients of an email can forward that email to an unlimited number of additional recipients with the simple click of the mouse. The sender has no control over how many people ultimately view the email he or she sends. If you don't want the email you send to be viewed by an unlimited number of people, you must send it to someone who you can trust will not forward it without your consent.

Verification

The nature of email makes it difficult to verify that the person who signs the email is the actual person who is sending the email. With regular mail, you can generally identify the sender by their handwriting, the signature, or the letterhead on which the correspondence is sent. However, you cannot identify an individual from the font type they use to create the email. Thus, it is possible to unwittingly correspond with a complete stranger who is pretending to be someone known to the user. There is software available on the market that can assist senders and recipients of emails with the identification process, such as the digital signature.

Unsolicited Email

Most Internet users are bombarded with numerous unsolicited junk email messages from businesses and individuals seeking to market their products, services and scams over the Internet. These emails are known as "spam." A business or individual will generally buy a list of email addresses from a third party, and then use software that allows them to send messages to everyone on the list within seconds. The harvesting of email addresses is generally automated. Spam email finds its way to new email addresses soon after they are used publicly for the first time.

Do not open unsolicited emails or attachments from unknown senders. You could be opening a virus that can interfere with your computer's operation, destroy important files stored on your computer, and reveal personal information stored on your computer. It is advisable to install and regularly update anti-virus software that will search your computer for viruses.

As set forth below, there are a number of methods designed to reduce the amount of unsolicited email messages.

Do Not Publicize Your Email Address

Since the individuals who compile the lists of email addresses harvest those addresses from the Internet, you should try not to display your email address publicly over the Internet. You should also request that your Internet service provider remove your name from membership directories that are posted on the Internet. In addition, you should try not to publish your email address in chat rooms and on websites.

Mask Your Email Address

Masking involves putting a word or phrase in your email address so that it will generally trick a harvesting computer program, but not a person. However, some newsgroup services or message boards won't allow you to mask your email address and some harvesting programs may be able to pick out common masks.

Use Two Email Addresses

Many websites require the user to provide their email address before they can sign up for online services or purchase products online. In that case, it might be prudent to use two email addresses and designate one for personal use and one for public use on the Internet. If you use chat rooms, use a screen name that's not associated with your email address. Consider using the screen name only for online chat.

Use Disposable Email Addresses

There are services that provide Internet users with "disposable" email addresses that forward email to the permanent email account. Then, if one of the disposable addresses begins to receive spam email, the user can turn it off without affecting their permanent address.

Create a Unique Email Address

Another method of trying to avoid being spammed is to create a unique email address. Your choice of email address may affect the amount of spam you receive. Some spammers use "dictionary attacks" to email many possible name combinations at large ISPs or email services, trying to come up with common names and variations to locate valid email addresses in order to compile a list. For example, marysmith@aol.com and variations of this email address are very easy for a spammer to validate. It is much more difficult to try and decode an email address that is randomly made up of numbers and letters.

Filter Junk Email

Many email systems have screening capabilities which allow the user to limit the amount of unsolicited commercial email that ends up in the user's inbox. Junk mail filters use certain criteria to filter out junk mail. For example, junk mail filters identify items such as font style, symbols, and phrasing to classify messages as junk mail.

The junk mail is then diverted to another folder, according to the user's preferences. Junk mail may be sent directly to the trash, or to a bulk email folder, where it generally remains for a certain amount of time before being automatically deleted. The user can view the contents of the folder at any time to make sure the junk mail filter is not eliminating emails that the user may want to receive.

Email Preference Service

Another way of reducing the amount of unsolicited commercial email is to register up for the email Preference Service (e-MPS) offered by the Direct Marketing Association (www.e-mps.org). All DMA members who wish to send unsolicited commercial email must delete from their email prospecting lists the names of any individuals who have registered their email address with e-MPS. The service is also available to non-DMA members.

Common Email Scams

Many consumers have lost thousands of dollars to these types of deceptive schemes. According to the FTC, many unsolicited email messages contain false information about the sender and/or misleading subject lines, and extravagant earnings or performance claims about goods and services. This widespread ability to disseminate false and misleading claims is the FTC's main concern with spam email. Some common deceptive spam email scams that an Internet user may encounter include illegal chain letters; work-at-home schemes; weight loss programs; credit repair offers; and advance-fee loan offers.

According to the FTC, another common scam designed to obtain personal financial information from the consumer involves email requests purportedly sent from the consumer's Internet service provider (ISP). The email request generally advises the consumer that "your account information needs to be updated" or that "the credit card you signed up with is invalid or expired and the information needs to be reentered to keep your account active." Consumers are advised not to respond to any such email request without first checking with their ISP.

Report Unsolicited Emails

The Federal Trade Commission (FTC) advises Internet users to forward unsolicited or deceptive email messages to their email address designated for this purpose (uce@ftc.gov). The FTC uses the unsolicited emails stored in this database to pursue law enforcement actions against those who send deceptive spam email. When making a complaint, it is important to include the full email header of the spam email. The information in the header makes it possible for the FTC to follow up on the complaint.

You should also send a copy of the unsolicited email to the abuse desk of their own Internet service provider (ISP). Include a copy of the spam, along with the full email header, and at the top of the message, state that you're complaining about being spammed. Forwarding your spam to your ISP lets them know about the spam problem on their system and helps them to stop it.

A complaint should also be made with the abuse desk of the sender's ISP. Most ISPs want to stop spammers who abuse their system. Include a copy of the message and the full email header information, and state that you're complaining about spam.

CHAPTER 7:
PROTECTING YOUR IDENTITY

SCOPE OF THE PROBLEM

Identity theft is a crime that occurs when someone wrongfully obtains and uses another individual's personal information in some way that involves fraud or deception, typically for financial gain. Identity theft is becoming the most expensive financial crime in the nation, costing consumers and the financial industry billions of dollars. Recent surveys estimate that nearly 10 million consumers are victimized by some form of identity theft each year. The stolen information was used to incur credit card debt, access bank accounts, and cause numerous personal and financial problems for the victim.

One may first become aware that they are the victim of identity theft when they notice that they are being billed for items they never purchased, or a credit account they never opened appears on their credit report. Many identity theft victims have reported that unauthorized persons have cleaned out their bank accounts, obtained credit in their name and, in some cases, have completely taken over their identities.

You may think that you diligently protect your personal information and, therefore, you are not a likely victim of identity theft. Unfortunately, intercepting your personal information is easier than you think. For example, identity thieves prey upon unsuspecting consumers while they are making their everyday transactions, such as banking and grocery shopping. Virtually every day-to-day transaction made requires the consumer to share some type of personal information, such as their name, address, phone number, bank account number, social security number, or credit card number, etc.

There are many schemes that identity thieves engage in once they obtain the victim's personal information, including but not limited to the following: (1) they open credit cards using the victim's personal identifying information and quickly exhaust the credit line; (2) they open bank accounts using the victim's information and write bad checks on the account; (3) they counterfeit checks or debit cards and drain the victim's bank accounts; and (4) they buy cars by taking out auto loans in the victim's name.

It is difficult, costly and time-consuming to undo all the damage identity theft can cause. It may be necessary to engage professional legal assistance because companies may be reluctant to accept the victim's representation that the account is fraudulent, and continue billing the victim and reporting delinquencies to credit reporting agencies.

MINIMIZING YOUR IDENTITY THEFT RISK

Although it may be impossible to completely prevent identity theft, you can minimize the risk by keeping careful track of your financial affairs and by cautiously guarding your personal information. When personal information is requested, ask how it is to be used and whether it will be shared with others. If possible, request that your information be kept confidential. Do not give out personal information over the telephone, through the mail, or over the Internet unless you have initiated the contact, and you know whom you are communicating with concerning the transaction. If you receive a telephone call or unsolicited mailing or Internet contact, do not reveal any personal information.

It is also important to be familiar with your billing cycles and follow up with creditors if statements are missing or late. Make sure that your billing address has not been changed without your knowledge. Make sure that the passwords you use for your credit cards and bank cards are not easily guessed, such as your date of birth or phone number, etc.

When shopping, try to take only those credit cards which you expect to use or need so as to minimize the amount of identification information available to potential thieves. Do not carry your social security card with you in your wallet or purse. If your wallet is lost or stolen, take immediate action to minimize the potential for theft of your personal information. Close your bank and credit card accounts immediately and open new accounts. Place a preliminary fraud alert on your credit profile.

You should also contact the Department of Motor Vehicles and any other institution that issued identification cards, and follow their procedures for replacing lost or stolen identification. Report the incident to your local police department. You must take immediate action because experienced identity thieves are aware that they have a limited time to run up your credit cards and misuse your identification, and they will act quickly.

Make sure your mail is safe by emptying your mailbox as soon as possible after delivery. Have the mail held at the post office when leaving for vacation.

Often, companies will send mailings to consumers that request the consumer to return postcards, such as warranty cards, customer surveys, etc. These postcards often contain personal information. Instead of returning the postcard, it is wiser to enclose the postcard in an envelope so that any personal information is not sent through the mail, and exposed to potential identity thieves.

When discarding trash that contains personal information, such as credit card receipts, bank statements, insurance information, etc., make sure these items are sufficiently shredded so that a potential identity thief cannot read the information. Also, before you dispose of your old computer, delete all of your personal information. Deleting files will not remove the files from your computer's hard drive; therefore, it is advisable to use a program that will overwrite the entire hard drive so your personal information cannot be retrieved.

In addition, find out who maintains the personnel files at your place of employment and verify that the information is secure. You should also make the same inquiries with any other entities that maintain a personal file on your behalf, such as your medical provider and insurance carrier. Ask that you be notified any time your personal information is requested by a third party so you can verify that the request is being made for a legitimate purpose that was authorized by you.

Protect Your Social Security Number

The social security number is the most sought after piece of personal identification by individuals seeking to create false identities. According to the Social Security Administration, identity crime accounts for over 80% of social security number misuse allegations according to the SSA.

You should be careful about sharing your number with anyone who asks for it, even when you are provided with a benefit or service. Identity thieves are often able to intercept one's social security number by stealing wallets, purses, and mail; through unsecured websites on the Internet; from business or personnel records at work or in the home; by sorting through trash; by posing as someone who legitimately needs this information; by buying personal information from inside sources, such as a store employee where you do your shopping.

Stolen and counterfeit social security numbers have been used to gain employment, obtain benefits and services, establish credit, and to commit crimes. Using another's social security number, identity thieves have applied for and/or received government benefits such as supplemental security income, disability insurance, worker's compensation benefits, unemployment benefits, and public assistance. This has caused significant losses to government programs, credit card companies, and banks, and has caused consumers considerable time and out-of pocket expenses trying to clear their name and resolve the problems arising from the theft.

There are a limited number of people who really require an individual's social security number for business purposes. For example, employers need an employee's social security number for wage and tax reporting purposes. Banks require a social security number in order to report taxable interest income. Many companies request an individual's social security number to perform credit checks before extending credit. However, some businesses request an individual's social security number merely for recordkeeping purposes. Thus, it may not be necessary to divulge your social security number to everyone who asks for it, although, in some instances, a company will decline providing you with a service you request if you refuse to give them your social security number.

Knowing why a company wants your social security number will make it easier to decide whether or not to share this information. The Federal Trade Commission (FTC) advises consumers to ask the following questions if a company asks for a social security number:

1. Why do you need my social security number?

2. How will my social security number be used?

3. What law requires me to give you my social security number?

4. What will happen if I don't give you my social security number?

According to the Social Security Administration, providing one's social security number, even if asked, is entirely voluntary. It is preferable to request companies that use your social security number merely for recordkeeping purposes, to provide you with an alternate number so that your social security number is not being circulated and subjected to potential interception by an identity thief. Alternate identification numbers offer some degree of protection of this most important piece of personal information.

RESOLVING YOUR IDENTITY THEFT PROBLEM

If you suspect that your personal information has been stolen and used in order to commit fraud, it is important to take immediate action.

You can expect to engage in numerous conversations with a variety of people, including customer service representatives, bank personnel, fraud investigators, government agencies, law enforcement agencies, etc.

It is advisable to keep a notebook with details of all of your contacts, including the dates, names, and substance of the conversations. It is virtually impossible to keep track of all of these contacts without a written record, which may prove helpful in resolving your unfortunate situation.

Identity theft may take many forms. However, in almost every identity theft case, there are basic steps the victim should take, as set forth below.

Credit Reporting Agencies

If you are the victim of identity theft, it is important to contact the fraud department of each of the three major credit reporting agencies as soon as possible and request them to place a "fraud alert" in your file, as well as a victim's statement asking that creditors call you before opening any new accounts or changing information on existing accounts. This can help prevent an identity thief from opening additional accounts in your name.

Following is the contact information for the fraud departments of each of the three major credit reporting agencies:

Equifax

Fraud Department
P.O. Box 740241
Atlanta, GA 30374-0241
Tel: 800-525-6285/TDD: 800-255-0056
Website: http://www.equifax.com

Experian

Fraud Department
P.O. Box 9532
Allen, TX 75013
Tel: 888-EXPERIAN (397-3742)/TDD: 800-972-0322
Website: http://www.experian.com

Transunion

Fraud Department
P.O. Box 6790
Fullerton, CA 92634-6790
Tel: 800-680-7289/TDD: 877-553-7803
Website: http://www.transunion.com

Credit Card Issuers

If your credit card is stolen, to minimize your liability, report the theft as soon as possible. Contact the fraud department of each credit card issuer for any accounts that have been tampered with or opened fraudulently. Some companies have toll-free numbers printed on their statements and 24-hour service to accept such emergency information. Note the name of the person you spoke with, and the date, time and substance of each conversation.

For your own protection, you should follow up your phone call with a letter to the credit card issuer. The letter should provide your credit card number, the date when you noticed your credit card was stolen, or that fraudulent accounts were opened in your name, and the date you reported the problem. This is particularly important because the consumer protection procedure for resolving errors on credit card billing statements requires that any disputes be in writing.

United States Postal Service

If the identity thief has stolen your mail for fraudulent purposes, e.g., to get new credit cards, bank and credit card statements, pre-screened credit offers or tax information, or if the identity thief has falsified change-of-address forms in order to divert billing statements, it should be reported to your local U.S. Postal Service Inspection Division immediately. You can find contact information for your local office on the U. S. Postal Inspection Service's website at: (http://www.usps.gov/websites/depart/inspect/).

You can also file a report electronically on the website. All information submitted through the website is transmitted via a secure server. If you prefer, you can mail your report and any correspondence to the following address:

U.S. Postal Inspection Service
Criminal Investigations Service Center
Attn: Mail Fraud
222 S. Riverside Plaza, Suite 1250
Chicago, Illinois 60606-6100

Banks

If the identity thief has tampered with your bank accounts, ATM card, or checks, close the accounts immediately and advise the appropriate bank authorities. Cancel all ATM cards and have new cards issued with new passwords that are not easily identifiable. You can contact the following major check verification companies to learn more about the services they provide in helping you track your stolen, forged or misused checks.

SCAN Check Verification Service
19803 North Creek Parkway
P.O. Box 1008
Bothell, WA 98041-1008
Tel: 1-800-262-7771

TeleCheck Services Inc.
P.O. Box 4451
Houston, TX 77210-4451
Tel: 1-800-710-9898
Fax: 713-332-9300
Website: www.telecheck.com

Investment Broker

If you believe that an identity thief has tampered with your securities investments or a brokerage account, immediately report the incident to your broker or account manager and to the Securities and Exchange Commission (SEC). You can also file a financial privacy complaint with the SEC if you believe your investment company has allowed someone to gain unauthorized access to your personal financial information, has improperly shared this information, or has failed to establish adequate safeguards to protect your personal financial information from unauthorized electronic access.

You can file a report electronically on the SEC website at: (www.sec.gov/complaint.shtml/). You should include as much information as possible regarding your complaint. All information submitted through the website is transmitted via a secure server.

If you prefer, you can mail or fax your complaint and any correspondence to the following address:

SEC Complaint Center
100 F Street NE
Washington, D.C. 20549-0213
Tel: 202-942-7040
Fax: 202-772-9295

Utilities/Telephone Service Provider

If an identity thief has established a utility or telephone account in your name; is using your calling card number, or is making unauthorized calls that seem to come from—and are billed to—your cellular phone, you should contact your service provider and immediately cancel the account and open a new account.

If a service provider is reluctant to remove fraudulent charges from your account, you may need to contact the office that governs their operations. For a local service provider, contact your state Public Utility Commission. For a long-distance telephone or cellular service provider, contact the Federal Communications Commission (FCC).

You can also file a complaint against your provider electronically on the FCC website at: (www.fcc.gov/cgb/complaints_general.html/).

If you prefer, you can mail your complaint and any correspondence to the following address:

Federal Communications Commission
445 12th Street SW
Washington, D.C. 20554
Tel: 1-888-CALL-FCC (1-888-225-5322)
Fax: 1-866-418-0232

If you mail your complaint, you should include the following information:

1. Your name, address and the telephone numbers involved with your complaint;

2. A telephone number where you can be reached during business hours;

3. Specific information about your complaint, including the name of the company involved with your complaint.

4. The names and telephone numbers of any company representatives that you contacted, the dates of contact, and the substance of any conversations;

5. A copy of the bill containing the charges you claim are fraudulent;

6. Any additional information that will support your complaint; and

7. The resolution you are seeking, e.g., removal of the charges and any associated penalties or fees.

Social Security Administration

The use of your social security number by someone else to obtain credit, loans, telephone accounts, or other goods and services should be reported immediately to the Federal Trade Commission (FTC), as set forth below.

THE FEDERAL TRADE COMMISSION (FTC)

The Federal Trade Commission (FTC) serves as a federal clearinghouse for complaints by victims of identity theft. Although the FTC does not have the authority to bring criminal cases, their mission is to help victims of identity theft by providing them with information to help resolve the financial and other problems that can result from identity theft.

Consumers can obtain further information as follows:

By Telephone:

1-877-ID THEFT (1-877-438-4338)
TDD: 1-866-653-4261

By Mail:

The Identity Theft Clearinghouse
Federal Trade Commission
600 Pennsylvania Avenue NW
Washington, DC 20580

Online:

(www.consumer.gov/idtheft/)

In addition, the FTC has developed the ID Theft Affidavit for victims of identity theft to complete and send to any company where a fraudulent account was opened in the victim's name by an identity thief. The ID Theft Affidavit simplifies the process of notifying companies by using one standard form.

The FTC ID Theft Affidavit and instructions for completing the form are set forth at Appendix 16.

CONSUMER SENTINEL

When an individual contacts the FTC with an Internet, telemarketing, identity theft or other fraud-related complaint, the FTC enters the information into Consumer Sentinel, the FTC's secure, online database. The database helps the FTC build cases and detect trends in consumer fraud and identity theft. Consumers can file a complaint regarding consumer fraud or identity theft at the Consumer Sentinel website: (http://www.consumer.gov/sentinel/)

Consumer Sentinel gives law enforcement access to over one million complaints, including consumer complaints from numerous Better Business Bureaus and the National Fraud Information Center. The Consumer Sentinel website also provides the consumer with helpful information, including the latest fraud trends and statistics, specific scams, and tips on how to recognize and avoid identity theft.

IDENTITY THEFT LEGISLATION

As set forth below, a number of federal and state laws have been passed in order to prevent identity theft.

The Identity Theft and Assumption Deterrence Act of 1998

In October 1998, Congress passed the Identity Theft and Assumption Deterrence Act to address the problem of identity theft. Under the Act, it is a federal crime to knowingly use a means of identification of another person with the intent to commit any unlawful activity that constitutes a violation of federal law, or that constitutes a felony under any applicable state or local law. Violations of the Act are investigated by federal investigative agencies such as the U.S. Secret Service, the FBI, and the U.S. Postal Inspection Service and prosecuted by the Department of Justice. In most instances, a conviction for identity theft carries a maximum penalty of 15 years imprisonment, a fine, and forfeiture of any personal property used or intended to be used to commit the crime.

The Identity Theft Penalty Enhancement Act

The Identity Theft Penalty Enhancement Act was enacted in 2004. The Act establishes penalties for aggravated identity theft as defined in the statute.

The Gramm-Leach-Bliley Act

In its effort to prevent identity theft, the Federal Trade Commission (FTC) recognized that many financial institutions' transactions with customers involve the collection of personal information, including names, addresses and phone numbers; bank and credit card account numbers; income and credit histories; and social security numbers. Under The Gramm-Leach-Bliley Act, financial institutions are prohibited from disclosing nonpublic personal information, including social security numbers, to non-affiliated third parties without first providing consumers with notice and the opportunity to opt out of the disclosure.

State Legislation

A number of states have passed legislation making identity theft a crime. Other states are considering such legislation. In states where there are no specific identity theft statutes, other state laws may govern such fraudulent practices. Most of the state statutes prohibiting identity theft generally criminalize the act of obtaining another's records or other personal information, without that person's authorization or consent, with the intent to defraud. The degree of the crime is usually measured by the dollar amount in financial loss to the victim.

CHAPTER 8:
HEALTH CARE RIGHTS

THE RIGHT TO HOSPITAL TREATMENT

Under the common law, a hospital has the right to refuse to admit or treat a person who comes in seeking admission or treatment, and the courts have generally deferred to the medical judgment of hospital personnel, and refused to require hospitals to use their medical resources for every person seeking treatment. Nevertheless, as further discussed below, there are circumstances under which the courts have held that the common law doctrine of no duty to admit or treat does not apply.

Emergency Situations

Hospitals are generally required to treat seriously injured or sick persons on an emergency basis, and their refusal to treat such people has resulted in the imposition of liability. However, the nature of an emergency is subjective and it is not always apparent whether a patient's condition actually constitutes an emergency.

In general, emergencies involve events which are sudden or unforeseen. However, even where an individual's condition is not in an emergency status at the time they arrive at the hospital, requiring that person to seek medical attention elsewhere may turn a non-emergency situation into an emergency. Thus, a hospital may also be required to prevent the occurrence of an emergency.

In addition, federal and state regulations generally require hospitals to treat children who have been abused or raped.

The Emergency Treatment and Active Labor Act (EMTALA)

Under the Emergency Treatment and Active Labor Act of 1986 (EMTALA)—also known as the "Anti-Dumping Act," medicare-provider hospitals are prohibited from transferring, discharging or refusing to

---

treat a patient solely because of his or her inability to pay for treatment where the hospital has the resources to provide the needed care. Hospitals that violate the EMTALA are subject to civil liabilities, including monetary sanctions.

Under the EMTALA, the hospital must provide an appropriate medical screening examination to any person seeking treatment or admission at an emergency department, to determine whether an emergency exists. If the individual refuses to submit to the medical examination, the hospital will have been deemed to have complied with the Act provided it adequately informs the individual of the risks associated with his or her refusal to be examined.

As defined by the Act, an emergency exists if the individual's medical condition could reasonably be expected to put the individual's health in serious jeopardy, or result in a serious impairment to bodily functions, or serious dysfunction of any bodily organ or part.

The Act also applies to pregnant women having contractions if there is not enough time to safely transfer the woman to another hospital before delivery without posing a threat to her health or safety, or the health and safety of her unborn child.

If the medical screening examination determines that the individual has an emergency medical condition, they may not be transferred or discharged unless their medical condition is stabilized.

An exception to the rule exists if the patient requests a transfer, in writing, after being thoroughly advised of the risks of the transfer and the hospital's obligation to treat the patient. In addition, another exception exists if a physician certifies that the medical benefits of the transfer outweigh the risks.

Discrimination

Many federal and state statutes prohibit unreasonable discrimination by hospitals in their refusal to admit or treat, despite the common law doctrine.

Discrimination on the Basis of Race, Color, Religion or National Origin

Hospitals are constitutionally prohibited from refusing to treat or admit a particular person due to their race, color, religion or national origin.

Discrimination on the Basis of Inability to Pay

Hospitals are not permitted to discriminate against patients based on their inability to pay for their treatment, particularly where the hospital receives federal assistance.

THE PATIENT'S RIGHT TO PARTICIPATE IN HEALTH CARE DECISIONS

As set forth below, every patient has the right and responsibility to fully participate in all decisions related to their health care.

The Right to Refuse Life-Sustaining Treatment

A patient has the right to refuse life-sustaining treatment. Life-sustaining treatment is defined as any medical treatment, procedure, or intervention that would serve only to prolong the dying process where the patient has a terminal illness or injury, or would serve only to maintain the patient in a condition of permanent unconsciousness. This includes commonly recognized life-sustaining measures, such as assisted ventilation and cardiopulmonary resuscitation (CPR), as well as any other medical treatments that may prolong life, such as kidney dialysis, surgical procedures, blood transfusions, heart medication, antibiotics, etc., regardless of whether the refusal may result in death.

Many states also set forth certain policy concerns—such as preservation of life and suicide prevention—to limit this right. The courts have looked to the circumstances concerning the patient when denial of the patient's rights is put in issue. Generally, if the patient is capable of recovery, the state's interest in preserving life has more merit than when the patient is on his or her death bed with no possibility of recovery. Further, the courts have distinguished between the act of suicide and the patient's right to die a natural death without being placed on life support.

The Right to Refuse Nutrition and Hydration

A patient has the right to refuse artificially provided nutrition and hydration, i.e., administration of food and water through a tube or intravenous line, where the patient is not required to chew or swallow voluntarily.

Do Not Resuscitate Order

A patient has the right to execute a Do-Not-Resuscitate Order (DNR). A DNR order is a physician's written order instructing health care providers not to attempt cardiopulmonary resuscitation (CPR) in the event the patient suffers cardiac or respiratory arrest.

The Right to Pain Management

A patient who experiences pain has the right to receive treatment to alleviate their pain even if the pain medication has the effect of hastening their death. A patient experiencing pain has the right to be advised as to:

1. The complete and current information about their condition;

2. The range of appropriate treatment options; and

3. The prognosis for their condition.

In addition, people experiencing pain are entitled to participate fully in the decisions affecting their care, and give truly informed consent to the treatment plan their doctor recommends. Regardless of the recommended treatment, the health care provider is also required to advise the patient of the risks and benefits of all available treatments, and the goals of treatment.

In addition, patients have the right to choose alternative treatments to manage their pain, including physical therapy, acupuncture, biofeedback/relaxation techniques, massage, chiropractic care, psychotherapy to help manage depression that may accompany chronic or intractable pain, hypnosis, and behavior modification.

INFORMED CONSENT

Along with a patient's right to participate in decisions about their health care is their right to understand what they are being told about their care and treatment. For example, the patient is entitled to a clear explanation of prescribed drugs, tests, treatments, and medical procedures.

The term "informed consent" refers to the requirement that a patient be apprised of the nature and risks of a medical procedure before the medical provider can validly claim exemption from liability for battery, or from responsibility for medical complications. Under the law, a health care provider cannot commence a medical procedure without first obtaining a patient's informed consent.

Manner of Consent

A patient gives consent to medical treatment either by: (1) express consent or (2) implied consent.

Express Consent

Express consent is obtained either in writing or orally. The health care provider is required to fully disclose all of the known and significant facts relevant to the procedure, in layperson's language, so that the patient can make an intelligent decision as to whether to go forward with the treatment. The following information should be provided to the patient to satisfy the informed consent requirement:

1. The diagnosis of the patient's condition and the prognosis without the proposed treatment;

2. The nature of the proposed treatment;

3. The goal to be achieved by the proposed treatment and the chance that the treatment will be successful;

4. The risks of the proposed treatment;

5. Any alternative treatments to the proposed treatment;

6. Identify:

(a) The health care provider(s) who discussed the proposed treatment with the patient;

(b) The health care provider(s) who will perform the proposed treatment;

7. Obtain consent to deviate from the proposed treatment in case of unforeseen circumstances.

8. Obtain consent to dispose of any tissue, organs or other body parts, if needed, for pathological study or research;

9. Acknowledgement that the patient's questions were fully discussed and adequately answered.

10. The patient's and/or legal guardian's signature, the signature of a witness, and the date, time, and location that the consent form was signed. If the patient is a minor, the parents may consent to the procedure, or, in the case of divorce, it is usually the parent having legal custody who may consent.

Where the health care provider has failed to obtain such consent, or where the quality of the consent is challenged, the patient may claim lack of informed consent for the procedure.

Implied Consent

Implied consent is obtained, for example, when a patient submits to a simple procedure. However, there is no implied consent where the procedure is invasive or non-customary.

Further, once a surgeon begins an internal surgical procedure, there is a presumption of implied consent if the surgeon does other necessary procedures in the process. This is so even if there are relatives in the vicinity who may be consulted. This is because the surgeon is not permitted to leave the operating room, once the surgery has begun, to obtain consent.

However, such implied consent only applies to necessary procedures. If the procedure is elective, the surgeon has the duty to delay until he receives the necessary consent for the additional surgery.

Implied consent also applies in emergency situations. If the emergency involves risk to the patient's life, or the patient is unable to give consent due to unconsciousness, coma or other incapacity, it has been held that the patient would have consented to the treatment if he or she were able, thus consent is implied in such situations.

Lack of Informed Consent

Lack of informed consent means that the patient did not fully understand what the health care provider was going to do, and was injured as a result of the health care provider's action. Further, the patient claims that if he had known what the health care provider planned to do, the patient would not have consented and, therefore, would have avoided the injury.

Absent an emergency, if the health care provider is able to ascertain, in advance of a surgical procedure, all of the possible alternatives available if an unexpected situation should arise during the operation, the patient has the right to be informed of the alternatives and given the chance to decide if those alternatives are acceptable before the health care provider proceeds with the procedure.

Informed Consent and Prescription Drugs

More often than not, a patient is prescribed medication without any details given to them about the particular medication. They simply take the often illegibly handwritten prescription to the pharmacy, have it filled, and start taking the drug according to the label's directions. However, patients have the right to know much more about the medicines that they are taking, and should take advantage of those rights.

Most problems associated with prescription drugs occur because the patient did not receive enough information concerning the medicine to use it properly. For example, they are unaware of what side effects to expect, or they improperly mix the medication with a food or drink, or another medication. The improper use of prescription medications can be deadly.

It is important to ask your medical provider every question you may have concerning a medication that is prescribed for you. A patient has the right to be informed about all aspects of their medical treatment, including the risks and benefits of the medicines prescribed; the potential side effects; and the necessity of monitoring the medication's effects. The patient also has the right to know the results of any tests that demonstrate whether or not the medication is working. For example, if the medical provider prescribes a cholesterol-reducing drug, the patient should be advised whether or not the medication is effectively reducing their cholesterol level.

The patient should also discuss with their medical provider all of the medicines that they are presently taking, including over-the-counter medicines, and whether there are any concerns about the interaction between those medicines with the medicine being prescribed. In particular, a patient has the right to the following information:

1. The name of the medicine and how it is intended to treat the patient's condition;

2. The dosage, frequency and duration prescribed, and whether there are refills available;

3. The foods, drinks, and other medicines that may negatively interact with the medication being prescribed.

4. The potential side effects of the medicine, and instructions on how to proceed should the patient experience those side effects;

5. An explanation of any terms or directions the patient does not understand.

6. A copy of any written information that may be available concerning the medication they are being prescribed.

The Food and Drug Administration (FDA) provides updated information about medication errors, including specific drugs that have been confused with one another. The information has been compiled based on voluntary reports received from consumers, doctors and other clinicians, as well as mandatory reports from manufacturers.

THE RIGHT TO EXECUTE ADVANCE DIRECTIVES

An "advance directive" is a general term that refers to one's oral and written instructions about their future medical care, in the event that they become unconscious or too sick to express their intentions. Executing an advance directive gives an individual the opportunity to make his or her own end-of-life health care decisions long after he or she has lost the capacity to do so. As long as the patient is able to express his or her own decisions, an advance directive will not be used and the patient has the right to accept or refuse any medical treatment regardless of the advance directive.

State Laws

All 50 states and the District of Columbia have laws recognizing the patient's right to execute some type of advance directive. The availability and scope of the particular advance directive varies from state to state, therefore, the reader is advised to check the law of his or her jurisdiction for specific provisions. Thus far, no state has challenged an individual's advance health care directives, and many states have enacted statutes that explicitly allow advance directives. The only health care decisions that have thus far been outlawed in all states, except Oregon, concern assisted suicide and euthanasia.

The Patient Self Determination Act of 1990

In order to make sure patients are aware of their rights to make their own end-of-life health care decisions, Congress enacted the Patient Self Determination Act of 1990 (PSDA), which requires hospitals to inform their patients about advance directives. Prior to enactment of the PSDA, many patients were unaware of their right to receive information that would help them make important decisions concerning their health care. The intent of the PSDA is to make sure patients are able to protect these rights in case they become at some point unable to do so, thus allowing the individual to maintain control of his or her own health care choices to the greatest extent possible.

Types of Advance Directives

A living will and a durable power of attorney for health care are the two primary types of advance directives in use today. A living will is a document that contains the patient's wishes concerning treatments he or she wants or does not want in case of incapacitation. A durable power of attorney for health care, also known as a health care proxy, is a document that appoints someone to be the patient's health care agent with the authority to make the patient's health care decisions when he or she is unable to do so.

THE FAMILY MEDICAL LEAVE ACT

In an increasing number of American families, both parents work outside the home. In addition, there are many families headed by a single working parent. Many families are taking care of young children and elderly parents, and working parents are faced with the possibility of losing their job if they take time from work to attend to a sick family member, to attend to their own health needs, or to care for a newborn or newly adopted baby.

On February 5, 1993, The Family and Medical Leave Act (FMLA) was enacted to address this problem. The goal of the FMLA is to help employees balance their work and family responsibilities by allowing them to take a reasonable amount of unpaid leave for certain family and medical reasons.

Following are some of the basic rights guaranteed employees under the FMLA:

The Right to Unpaid Leave

The most important provision of the FMLA is the employee's right to unpaid job-protected leave under certain circumstances. The FMLA provides that a "covered employer" must grant an "eligible employee" up to 12 weeks of unpaid, job-protected leave per year. If the employee has earned or accrued paid leave, such leave may be substituted instead of unpaid leave. If the employee does not elect to substitute paid leave, the employer may require the use of accrued paid leave. In certain cases, FMLA leave may be taken on an intermittent basis—i.e., in segments—rather than all at once, or the employee may work a part-time schedule, known as a reduced leave schedule.

Under the FMLA, the circumstances which trigger the employee's right to take FMLA leave include: (1) the birth of an employee's son or daughter and care of the newborn; (2) placement of a child with the employee for adoption or foster care; (3) the employee's own serious health condition which makes the employee unable to perform the functions of his or her job; or (4) the need to care for an immediate family member—i.e., a child, spouse, or parent—with a serious health condition.

The Right to Maintenance of Group Health Benefits

Another important provision of the FMLA is the employee's right to have their health benefits maintained while on FMLA leave as if the employee had continued to work instead of taking the leave. In addition, the employer must continue to pay whatever share of the employee's health care premium the employer was paying prior to the employee's leave period, and if an employee was paying all or part of the premium payments prior to taking leave, the employee must continue to pay his or her share during their leave period. The employer may recover its share only if the employee does not return to work for a reason other than the serious health condition of the employee or the employee's immediate family member, or another reason beyond the employee's control.

The Right to Job Protection

Under the FMLA, an employee generally has the right to return to the same position or an equivalent position with equivalent pay, benefits and working conditions at the conclusion of the leave. In fact, taking FMLA leave cannot result in the loss of any employee benefit that accrued prior to the start of the leave.

The employer has the right to 30 days advance notice from the employee that he or she will be taking FMLA leave, if practicable. In addition, the employer may require an employee to submit certification from a health care provider to substantiate that the leave is due to the serious health condition of the employee or the employee's immediate family member. Failure to comply with these requirements may result in a delay in the start of FMLA leave.

Interference With FMLA Rights

An employer is prohibited from interfering with, restraining, or denying the exercise of any rights provided by the FMLA. Any violations of the FMLA or its regulations constitute "interfering with, restraining, or denying" the exercise of rights provided by the FMLA.

Interfering with the exercise of an employee's rights would include, for example, not only refusing to authorize FMLA leave, but discouraging an employee from using such leave. Interference would also include manipulation by a covered employer to avoid responsibilities under the FMLA, e.g., reducing hours available to work in order to avoid employee eligibility.

In addition, employees cannot waive—nor may employers induce employees to waive—their rights under the FMLA. For example, employees, or their collective bargaining representatives, cannot "trade off" the right to take FMLA leave against some other benefit offered by the employer.

Further, an employer is prohibited from discriminating against employees or prospective employees who have used FMLA leave, and cannot use the taking of FMLA leave as a negative factor in employment actions, such as hiring, promotion, or disciplinary action.

An employer is also prohibited from discharging or in any other way discriminating against any person for filing a complaint against the employer concerning any violations of the FMLA, as set forth below.

Remedies for FMLA Violations

If an employee's rights under the FMLA are violated by his or her employer, the employee may (1) file a complaint against their employer with the Secretary of Labor; or (2) file a private lawsuit against their employer. If an employee decides to file a private lawsuit, it must be filed within two years after the last action that the employee contends was in violation of the FMLA, or three years if the violation was willful.

If it is shown that the employer violated one or more provisions of the FMLA, the employee may receive the wages, employment benefits, or other compensation that was denied or lost to the employee due to the violation. If there was no tangible loss—e.g., when the violation was an unlawful denial of FMLA leave—the employee may recover any actual monetary loss suffered as a direct result of the violation. This may include the cost of providing care, up to a sum equal to 12 weeks of wages for the employee, with interest calculated at the prevailing rate.

In addition, the employee may also recover a reasonable attorney's fee, reasonable expert witness fees, and other costs of the action from the employer in addition to any judgment awarded by the court. However, if the employer's violation was made in good faith, and the employer had reasonable grounds for believing that no violation occurred, the court may reduce the employee's monetary award.

The employee may also obtain appropriate equitable relief, such as employment, reinstatement and promotion.

MEDICAL RECORDS PRIVACY

Information concerning an individual's medical condition is of interest to a number of entities for a variety of reasons, including insurance carriers, employers, health care providers, government agencies, and law enforcement. Technological advances have made accessing, disseminating and sharing an individual's medical records relatively easy and swift. However, without legal safeguards, there is the potential for virtually unlimited access to an individual's medical records without his or her knowledge or consent.

The danger in allowing the unauthorized dissemination of an individual's medical records is that certain entities may use this information to the patient's detriment. For example, insurance carriers may refuse to issue life and health insurance policies to those individuals they deem as risks based on their medical history, and employers may be unwilling to employ individuals who they deem are unhealthy based on their medical records.

Unfortunately, there is presently no comprehensive national policy ensuring the privacy of an individual's medical records, although some states have enacted laws in an attempt to protect their citizens from a breach of their privacy. The amount of privacy your medical records receive depends on where the records are located and the reason the information was gathered.

Generally, access to an individual's medical records occurs when the individual gives their consent for another to obtain those records. In some cases, this is necessary—e.g., when applying for an insurance policy; pre-employment testing; and to support an application for disability or workers compensation benefits.

The Health Insurance Portability and Accountability Act (HIPAA)

In an effort to address this problem, Congress passed the federal Health Insurance Portability and Accountability Act (HIPAA) which became effective in 2003. HIPAA established standards for patient privacy in all 50 states. The problem is that HIPAA only applies to medical records maintained by health care providers, health plans, and health clearing-houses, and only if the facility maintains and transmits records in electronic form.

Strategies to Limit Access to Medical Records

Although HIPAA provides some protection, it does not solve the medical records privacy problem. Unfortunately, there still exists a lot of patient health-related information beyond what HIPAA covers. Thus, an individual must employ strategies to limit access to their medical records, as follows:

1. When completing an authorization for the release of medical records, limit the amount of information to be released by inserting specific terms in the document.

2. Discuss your privacy concerns with your physician. If you want your physician to keep a certain medical condition confidential, pay for the visit out-of-pocket and revoke your consent to released medical information to your insurance carrier concerning the particular condition.

3. Ask your health care provider to release only as much information as an authorization requires instead of copying and providing all of your medical records, e.g. date limitations, information concerning a specific condition, etc.

Patient's Right to Access Medical Records

Under the HIPAA, a patient has the right to access their own medical records. Health care providers are required to allow an individual access to their medical records, and to provide information advising the patient how they can obtain copies of their medical records.

In addition to HIPAA, about half the states have laws that allow patients or their designated representatives to access medical records. Further, patients who receive care in a federal medical facility have the right to obtain their medical records under the federal Privacy Act of 1974.

Your request for medical records should be made in writing and sent to the medical records office of your health care provider. State laws usually allow health care providers to charge a "reasonable" fee for copying the records.

If you are denied access to your medical records, you can file a complaint with the U.S. Department of Health and Human Service's Office of Civil Rights. Your state's medical privacy law might also enable you to file a complaint with state regulators.

CHAPTER 9:
YOUR RIGHTS AS A TENANT

THE LANDLORD/TENANT RELATIONSHIP

A landlord is the owner of rental property that is leased to another person, known as a "tenant." The landlord is also referred to as the "lessor" of the rental property. The rental property is generally a house, an apartment, a condominium, co-op, or room. The tenant is the individual who has been given the right to use and occupy the rental property pursuant to the terms and conditions of the lease, also referred to as a "rental agreement." The tenant is referred to as the "lessee" of the rental property.

The landlord leases the property to the tenant in exchange for the payment of money, known as rent. The tenant obtains the right to the exclusive use and possession of the rental property during the lease period for the purpose of making it his or her home.

The law that governs the relationship between the landlord and the tenant and the rental of residential property is simply known as "landlord-tenant law." Landlord-tenant law is derived from both statutory law and the common law—i.e., judge-made law.

A table of state tenants' rights laws is set forth in Appendix 17.

THE RIGHT TO FAIR HOUSING

Federal, state and local fair housing laws provide protection to prospective tenants against housing discrimination. It is illegal for a landlord to refuse to rent to a tenant on the basis of group characteristics specified by law that are not closely related to the business needs of the landlord. In general, discrimination based on the following factors have been deemed illegal under various federal and state statutes:

1. Race

2. Color

3. Religion

4. Gender

5. Marital status

6. National origin

7. Ancestry

8. Familial status

9. Mental disability

10. Physical disability

11. Sexual orientation

Further, although it is illegal for landlords to discriminate against families with children, specially designated senior citizen housing may set a minimum age requirement for all occupants.

The reader is advised to check the law of his or her own jurisdiction concerning the categories of discrimination that are deemed illegal, as some states may afford greater coverage than others.

Exceptions

Owner-occupied, single-family homeowners who rent out a single room in the home to a lodger, where there are no other lodgers living in the household, are not subject to some of the restrictions on illegal discrimination. Nevertheless, the owner cannot make oral or written statements, or use notices or advertisements that indicate any preference, limitation, or discriminatory practice. However, a person in a single-family home seeking a roommate may express a gender preference if there will be common living areas.

Remedies

A victim of discrimination may file a housing discrimination complaint with the United States Department of Housing and Urban Development (HUD). HUD will investigate the complaint and take action if warranted. If the discrimination is a violation of a state fair housing law, the tenant may wish to file a complaint with the state agency in charge of enforcing the law. Instead of filing a complaint with HUD or a state agency, the complainant may choose to file a lawsuit directly in federal or state court.

An individual who is subjected to illegal housing discrimination is generally entitled to recover damages, which may include one or more of the following:

1. Monetary compensation for actual damages, including reimbursement for expenses incurred in seeking alternative housing;

2. The right to obtain the desired housing;

3. Any other damages suffered which are provable; and

4. Legal fees and costs.

Victims of housing discrimination may obtain further information and assistance by contacting HUD. In addition, many jurisdictions have their own local fair housing organizations and consumer protection agencies that can be a source of further information. Legal aid organizations may also provide free advice and/or representation to persons who qualify for services. There are also private attorneys who specialize in housing discrimination litigation.

The Federal Fair Housing Act

The Fair Housing Act prohibits housing discrimination based on one's race, color, national origin, religion, sex, family status, or disability, and provides that no one may take any of the following actions if based on these factors:

1. Refuse to rent or sell housing;

2. Refuse to negotiate for housing;

3. Make housing unavailable;

4. Deny a dwelling;

5. Set different terms, conditions or privileges for sale or rental of a dwelling;

6. Provide different housing services or facilities;

7. Falsely deny that housing is available for inspection, sale, or rental;

8. For profit, persuade owners to sell or rent, an activity known as blockbusting;

9. Deny anyone access to, or membership in, a facility or service related to the sale or rental of housing;

10. Threaten, coerce, intimidate or interfere with anyone who is exercising a fair housing right, or assisting others who exercise that right; or

11. Advertise or make any statement that indicates a limitation or preference based on race, color, national origin, religion, gender, familial status, or handicap.

Filing a HUD Complaint

If you think a landlord has broken a federal fair housing law, you can file a fair housing complaint with HUD's Fair Housing Enforcement

Center. Complaints must be filed within one year of the alleged discriminatory act. If HUD determines that your state or local agency has the same fair housing powers as HUD, it will refer your complaint to that agency for investigation. You will be notified of the referral. That agency must begin work on your complaint within 30 days or HUD may reclaim the complaint.

When filing a complaint with HUD, be prepared to give the following information:

1. Your name and address;

2. The name and address of the person you claim violated the law;

3. The address of the rental property;

4. The date when the incident occurred; and

5. A short description of the circumstances.

HUD will notify you when it receives your complaint. HUD will also notify the alleged violator—called the "respondent"—and permit that person to submit an answer to the complaint. HUD will then investigate your allegations, and determine whether there is reasonable cause to believe the Fair Housing Act has been violated.

HUD will then normally appoint a mediator to negotiate with the landlord and reach a settlement, also known as a "conciliation." A conciliation agreement must protect both you and the public interest. If an agreement is reached, HUD will take no further action on your complaint unless it has reasonable cause to believe that the conciliation agreement is breached. In that case, HUD will generally recommend that the Attorney General file suit.

If HUD is unable to negotiate a settlement, an administrative hearing may be held to determine whether discrimination has occurred. If the case does proceed to an administrative hearing, HUD attorneys will litigate the case on your behalf. An Administrative Law Judge (ALJ) will consider your evidence and any evidence provided by the respondent landlord. If the ALJ decides that discrimination has occurred, the ALJ may order the landlord to:

1. Pay compensation for actual damages, including humiliation, pain and suffering;

2. Provide injunctive or other equitable relief, e.g., make the housing available;

3. Pay the Federal Government a civil penalty to vindicate the public interest; and/or

4. Pay reasonable attorney's fees and costs.

If there is noncompliance with the ALJ's order, HUD may seek temporary relief, enforcement of the order or a restraining order in a United States Court of Appeals. In addition, the Attorney General may file a suit in a Federal District Court if there is reasonable cause to believe a pattern or practice of housing discrimination is occurring.

A HUD Fair Housing Discrimination Complaint form is set forth in Appendix 18.

THE WARRANTY OF HABITABILITY

Under the warranty of habitability, it is generally required that the landlord ensure, before renting, that the property is habitable—i.e., fit for occupation by humans—and in substantial compliance with building and health codes. In addition, landlords are generally required to maintain the rental property in a habitable condition during the rental period. Minor code violations not affecting habitability, or the failure to undertake minor repairs or cosmetic alterations would not likely violate the implied warranty of habitability.

Common defects which may render rental property uninhabitable include but are not limited to:

1. Lack of weather protection, such as broken windows and leaking rooftops;

2. Failure to provide adequate plumbing facilities, including hot and cold running water;

3. Failure to provide an adequate sewage disposal system;

4. Failure to provide adequate heat;

5. Failure to provide adequate lighting;

6. Failure to provide a working stove and refrigerator; and

7. Failure to keep the building clean and free from trash and infestation.

If the landlord neglects the responsibility to maintain the rental property, the tenant should put the landlord on written notice of his or her duty to do so. The letter should detail the repairs that need to be made. In addition, the tenant should take photographs of any visible damage. The tenant should keep one copy of the letter and mail the original to the landlord by certified mail with a return receipt to establish that the landlord received the letter. If after a reasonable period of time the landlord still neglects to make the repairs, there are several courses of action the tenant may take, as discussed below.

The Right to Repair and Deduct

Under the "repair and deduct" method, the tenant deducts the amount of money necessary to complete the repairs from his or her rent payment. In order to justify using this remedy, the tenant should only make repairs that breach the warranty of habitability or otherwise threaten the tenant's health and safety.

It is important to keep all repair receipts to justify the amount deducted from the rent. In addition, the tenant should send written notice to the landlord, by certified mail-return receipt requested, explaining his or her reasons for deducting the repair money from the rent.

The tenant runs the risk of a lawsuit by the landlord for nonpayment of rent or eviction, and should be prepared to defend his or her right to deduct the repair money from the rent. Nevertheless, the landlord is generally prohibited from taking any action that may be deemed retaliatory.

The Right to Withhold Rent

A tenant may choose to withhold all or part of the rent if the landlord refuses to undertake the necessary repairs. Again, the repairs must be serious enough to render the property uninhabitable or threaten the tenant's health and safety. Under this remedy, the rent is not paid until the landlord makes the necessary repairs. The withheld rent should be maintained in an account. The landlord should be advised, in writing, that the rent money is being held in escrow until the repairs are made.

As with the "repair and deduct" remedy above, rent withholding also subjects the tenant to the risk that the landlord will sue for nonpayment of rent or eviction.

The Right to Abandon the Property

A tenant is generally entitled to abandon the rental property without penalty if it is rendered uninhabitable due to the landlord's failure to make necessary repairs. When rental property is uninhabitable, it creates a condition known as "constructive eviction"—i.e., the condition of the property is such that the tenant is unable to enjoy full use and possession and has thus, as a practical matter, been "evicted" from the property. However, to be constructively evicted, the defects must be serious enough to breach the warranty of habitability or otherwise render the rental property unsafe or unhealthy.

If the tenant must abandon the property under these circumstances, he or she is no longer liable for rent under the lease, and is still entitled to a refund of the security deposit. The tenant should send written notice to the landlord, by certified mail-return receipt requested, explaining his or her reasons for moving.

THE RIGHT TO QUIET ENJOYMENT

A tenant is entitled to privacy, exclusive possession, and the right to "quiet enjoyment" of the rental property. Thus, a landlord's right of entry is limited. In general, a landlord can only enter the rental property under the following circumstances:

1. In case of an emergency;

2. To make necessary repairs or to assess the need for repairs;

3. To show the property to prospective buyers or tenants; and

4. Upon abandonment of the rental property by the tenant.

Unless there is an emergency, or the tenant has abandoned the premises, the landlord is generally required to give the tenant advance notice—e.g., at least 24 hours—before entering the rental property for any other purpose.

Many states also allow a landlord the right of entry during a tenant's extended absence, in order to maintain the property as needed. However, a landlord may not enter merely to check up on the tenant and the rental property.

In general, you cannot refuse to let the landlord into the apartment without good reason. For example, you can require advance notice, or prevent the landlord from entering the apartment during unusual hours—e.g., in the middle of the night—unless there is an emergency. If you prevent the landlord from entering the apartment without good reason, the landlord may have the right to terminate your lease and start eviction proceedings, or take you to court to obtain a court order allowing the landlord the right to enter the premises.

In addition, you cannot circumvent the landlord's right of entry by changing the locks on the doors. Even if you have the right to change the locks, you are generally required to provide the landlord with a set of keys to the new lock.

THE RIGHT TO SAFE PREMISES

Dangerous or Defective Conditions

A landlord may be liable to the tenant or third parties for injuries caused by dangerous or defective conditions on the rental property. In order to hold the landlord responsible, however, the tenant must be able to prove that the landlord was negligent, and that the landlord's negligence caused an injury. The tenant must be able to show that:

1. The landlord had control over the problem that caused the injury;

2. The accident was foreseeable;

3. Repairing the problem would not have been unreasonably expensive or difficult;

4. A serious injury was the probable consequence of not fixing the problem;

5. The landlord failed to take reasonable steps to avoid the accident;

6. The landlord's failure to repair the problem caused the tenant's accident; and

7. The tenant was genuinely hurt as a result of the landlord's negligence.

An injured person may file a personal injury lawsuit seeking damages for medical bills, lost earnings, pain and other physical suffering, permanent physical disability and disfigurement and emotional distress.

Criminal Activities

Landlords are generally responsible for keeping the rental property safe and secure for tenants and guests—e.g., making sure that doors and windows have proper locks and common areas are well-lit, etc. Most states hold landlords legally responsible to some degree in protecting their tenants from burglars and other criminals, as well as from the criminal actions of co-tenants and employees.

The failure to make a reasonable assessment of the crime potential of the area, and follow up with security measures designed to eliminate or reduce the threat of safety, may subject the landlord to a greater degree of legal liability if a tenant is injured as a result of the landlord's negligence.

THE SECURITY DEPOSIT REFUND

A security deposit is a fee, in addition to the first month's rent, which the landlord requires the tenant to pay before moving into the rental property. The purpose of the security deposit is to protect the landlord in case the tenant damages the property during occupancy, or if the tenant moves out without paying the rent.

State laws require the landlord to hold the tenant's security deposit in a bank account, and the tenant must be given information concerning the name of the bank where the funds are being held. Interest earned on the funds generally belongs to the landlord unless there is a written agreement to the contrary, or if the applicable law requires the interest to be turned over to the tenant.

Many leases contain a provision that prohibits the tenant from "committing waste" in the rental property. This basically means that the tenant has the duty to keep the rental property clean, and shall not intentionally or negligently cause damage to the property. Landlords are permitted to make deductions from the tenant's security deposit if the rental property is damaged or excessively dirty, however, deductions cannot be made for reasonable and ordinary wear and tear.

Basically, a landlord may charge a tenant for repairs that are necessary to restore the rental property to the condition it was in when the tenant took possession. The landlord may also charge a tenant for cleaning if it is determined that the rental property was left in an excessively dirty condition, although such a determination is somewhat subjective and may lead to a dispute with the landlord that ends up in small claims court.

If a tenant moves out without owing any rent, and without causing any damage to the rental property above normal wear and tear, he or she is entitled to a refund of the entire security deposit. Many states require landlords to provide the tenant with a detailed list of all deductions taken from a security deposit, whether for unpaid rent or for repairs.

The balance of the security deposit, after the deductions are made, is then returned to the tenant, usually within a prescribed period of time. In most states, the security deposit must be returned within 14 to 30 days after the tenant vacates the apartment. Depending on the state, if the landlord does not send the refund and/or a statement of deductions to the tenant within the applicable time period, the landlord may not be entitled to keep any portion of the security deposit.

A table of state rules for returning security deposits is set forth in Appendix 19.

EVICTION

If a landlord wants to remove a tenant, there are legally prescribed methods which must be followed. The landlord is not entitled to physically remove the tenant and his or her belongings from the rental property, nor can the landlord make living conditions uninhabitable to try and force the tenant to leave. These types of tactics—generally known as "self-help" measures—are illegal and may result in the landlord having to pay the tenant's damages.

The landlord is usually required to serve the tenant with some type of written notice before terminating the tenancy. Where there is a valid lease, the landlord cannot terminate the tenancy unless he or she has just cause to do so, e.g., the tenant violates a term contained in the lease. If the landlord believes that he or she has just cause to evict the tenant, the landlord must give the tenant the amount of notice required under the applicable statute.

Illegal Landlord Actions

A landlord is prohibited from trying to make a tenant abandon the rental property, or from retaliating against a tenant who complains or takes legal action against a landlord. If a landlord takes any illegal actions against the tenant, the landlord may be held liable to the tenant for damages, including legal fees and costs. The following landlord actions have been deemed illegal:

Self-Help Eviction

As set forth above, self-help as a method of eviction is generally restricted. Some states do not even allow it for tenants who have held over after the end of a lease. Thus, a landlord is prohibited from locking a tenant out of the rental property, e.g., by changing the locks. This is so even if the tenant's rent is in arrears. The landlord's only legal recourse is to begin eviction proceedings.

Utility Shutoffs

A landlord is prohibited from shutting off the utilities to a tenant's rental property for any reason. Further, if the landlord intentionally refuses to pay the utility bills so that the service is terminated, this may also constitute an illegal action.

Removing Tenant Property

A landlord is prohibited from removing a tenant's property from the rental property unless the tenant has abandoned the rental. It would be illegal for the landlord to remove a tenant's property for any other reason.

Residential Evictions Under the Bankruptcy Abuse Prevention and Consumer Protection Act of 2005

The Bankruptcy Abuse Prevention and Consumer Protection Act of 2005 affects the procedures landlords must follow when dealing with a tenant who has filed for bankruptcy. Generally, if a tenant has filed for either Chapter 7 or Chapter 13 bankruptcy and is behind in the rent, becomes unable to pay the rent, or violates another term of the tenancy that would justify a termination, a landlord cannot deliver a termination notice or proceed with an eviction.

This prohibition is known as the "automatic stay," and it means that landlords must go to the federal bankruptcy court and ask the judge to "lift"—i.e., remove the stay. In most cases, the judge will lift the stay within a matter of days and the landlord can proceed with a termination and eviction.

The automatic stay does not apply, however, if the eviction lawsuit is completed and the landlord obtained a judgment for possession before the tenant filed for bankruptcy. In this situation, under the Act, landlords can generally proceed with the eviction without having to go to court and ask for the stay to be lifted.

Depending on the state, under very limited circumstances, a tenant can stop an eviction based upon non-payment of rent even if the landlord obtained a judgment before the tenant filed for bankruptcy.

APPENDIX 1:
DIRECTORY OF NATIONAL CONSUMER ORGANIZATIONS

ORGANIZATION	ADDRESS	TELEPHONE	FAX	EMAIL	WEBSITE
AARP Consumer Protection Unit	601 E Street NW, Washington, DC 20049	202-434-2222	202-434-6470	n/a	www.aarp.org/
Alliance Against Fraud in Telemarketing and Electronic Commerce (AAFTEC) National Consumers League	1701 K St. NW, Suite 1200, Washington, DC 20006	202-835-3323	202-835-0747	info@nclnet.org	www.fraud.org/aaft/aaftinfo.htm/
American Council on Consumer Interests (ACCI)	415 South Duff Ave., Suite C, Ames, IA 50010-6600	515-956-4666	515-233-3101	info@consumerinterests.org	www.consumerinterests.org/
American Council on Science and Health (ACSH)	1995 Broadway, 2nd Floor, New York, NY 10023-5860	212-362-7044	212-362-4919	acsh@acsh.org	www.acsh.org/
Center for Auto Safety, (CAS)	Washington, DC 20009	202-328-7700	n/a	n/a	www.autosafety.org/
Center for Science in the Public Interest (CSPI)	1875 Connecticut Ave. NW, Suite 300, Washington, DC 20009	202-332-9110	202-265-4954	cspi@cspinet.org	www.cspinet.org/

ORGANIZATION	ADDRESS	TELEPHONE	FAX	EMAIL	WEBSITE
Center for the Study of Services/Consumers' Checkbook Magazine	1625 K St. NW, 8th Floor, Washington, DC 20006	202-347-7283	n/a	support@checkbook.org	www.checkbook.org/
Certified Financial Planner Board of Standards, Communication and Consumer Services	1670 Broadway, Suite 600, Denver, CO 80202-4809	303-830-7500	303-860-7388	mamil@cfp-board.org	www.CFP-Board.org/
Coalition Against Insurance Fraud	1012 14th St. NW, Suite 200, Washington, DC 20005	202-393-7330	202-318-9189	info@insurancefraud.org	www.InsuranceFraud.org/
Congress Watch	215 Pennsylvania Ave. SE, Washington, DC 20003	202-546-4996	202-547-7392	congresswatch@citizen.org	www.citizen.org/congress/
Consumer Action	San Francisco, CA 94105	415-777-9635	415-777-5267	info@consumer-action.org	www.consumer-action.org/
Consumer Federation of America (CFA)	1620 I Street, Suite 200, Washington, DC 20006	202-387-6121	202-265-7989	cfa@consumerfed.org	www.consumerfed.org/
Consumer Reports	Yonkers, NY 10703-1057	914-378-2000	914-378-290	n/a	www.consumerreports.org/
Consumers for World Trade (CWT)	1001 Connecticut Ave. N.W., Suite 1110, Washington, DC 20036	202-293-2944	202-293-0495	cwt@cwt.org	www.cwt.org/

Consumers Union	101 Truman Avenue, Yonkers, NY 10703-1057	914-378-2000	914-378-2900	n/a	www. consumersunion. org/
Consumer Policy Institute	1101 17th Street NW, Suite 500, Washington, DC 20036	202-462-6262	202-265-9548	n/a	n/a
Families USA	1201 New York Avenue NW, Suite 1100, Washington, DC 20005	202-628-3030	202-347-2417	info@familesusa. org	www.familiesusa. org/
The Federation of American Consumers and Travelers (FACT)	P.O. Box 104, Edwardsville, IL 62025	1-800-USA-FACT	202-250-5811	cservice@usafact. org	www.usafact.org/
Funeral Consumers Alliance	33 Patchen Road, South Burlington, VT 05403	802-865-8300	802-865-2626	info@funerals.org	www.funerals.org/
HALT: An Organization of Americans for Legal Reform	1612 K St. NW, Suite 510, Washington, DC 20006	202-887-8255	202-887-9699	halt@halt.org	www.halt.org/
Health Research Group (HRG)	Washington, DC 20009	202-588-1000	n/a	pcmail@citizen.org	www. citizen.org/hrg/
Hearing Loss Association of America	7910 Woodmont Ave., Suite 1200, Bethesda, MD 20814	301-657-2248	301-913-9413	info@hearingloss. org	www.heearingloss. org/
Jump$tart Coalition for Personal Financial Literacy	919 18th St. NW, Suite 300, Washington, DC 20006	202-466-8604	202-223-0321	info@ jumpstartcoalition. org	www.jumpstart. org/

ORGANIZATION	ADDRESS	TELEPHONE	FAX	EMAIL	WEBSITE
National Association of Consumer Agency Administrators (NACAA)	Two Brentwood Commons, Suite 150, 750 Old Hickory Blvd., Brentwood, TN 37027	615-371-6125	615-369-6225	nacaa@nacaa.net	www.nacaa.net/
National Coalition for Consumer Education	1701 K St. NW, Suite 1200, Washington, DC 20006	202-835-3323	202-835-0747	n/a	www.nclnet.org/
National Community Reinvestment Coalition (NCRC)	Washington, DC 20005-2112	202-628-8866	202-628-9800	member@ncrc.org	www.ncrc.org/
National Consumer Law Center (NCLC)	77 Summer St., 10th Floor, Boston, MA 02111-1006	617-542-8010	617-542 8028	consumerlaw@nclc.org	www.consumerlaw.org/
The National Consumer Protection Technical Resource Center	1155 21st Street NW, Suite 202, Washington, DC 20036	1-877-808-2468	202-331-9334	info@smpresource.org	www.smpresource.org/
National Consumers League	1701 K St. NW, Suite 1200, Washington, DC 20006	202-835-3323	202-835-0747	n/a	www.nclnet.org

National Council on the Aging (NCOA)	300 D St. SW, Suite 801, Washington, DC 20024	202-479-1200	202-479-0735	info@ncoa.org	www.ncoa.org/
National Fraud Information Center/ Internet Fraud Watch	Washington, DC 20006	1-800-876-7060	202-835-0767	n/a	www.fraud.org/
Public Citizen, Inc.	1600 20th St. NW, Washington, DC 20009	202-588-1000	n/a	rpleatman@citizen.org	www.citizen.org/
Society of Consumer Affairs Professionals in Business (SOCAP)	675 North Washington St., Suite 200, Alexandria, VA 22314	703-519-3700	703-549-4886	socap@socap.org	www.socap.org/
U.S. Public Interest Research Group (U.S. PIRG)	218 D St. SE, Washington, DC 20003-1900	202-546-9707	202-546-2461	uspirg@pirg.org	www.uspirg.org/

SOURCE: The Federal Citizen Information Center of the U.S. General Services Administration

APPENDIX 2:
DIRECTORY OF STATE CONSUMER PROTECTION AGENCIES

STATE	ADDRESS	TELEPHONE NUMBER	FAX	EMAIL	WEBSITE
Alabama	Consumer Protection Division, Office of the Attorney General, 11 S. Union Street, Montgomery, AL 36130	334-242-7335	n/a	n/a	www.ago.state.al.us/
Alaska	Consumer Protection Section, Office of the Attorney General, 1031 W. 4th Avenue, Suite 200, Anchorage, AK 99501	907-269-5100	907-276-8554	n/a	www.law.state.ak.us/
Arizona	Financial Fraud Division, Office of the Attorney General, 1275 W. Washington St., Phoenix, AZ 85007	602-542-5025	602-542-4085	n/a	www.azag.gov/
Arkansas	Consumer Protection Division, Office of the Attorney General, 323 Center St., Suite 200, Little Rock, AR 72201	501-682-2007	501-682-8118	consumer@ag.state.ar.us	www.ag.state.ar.us/

STATE	ADDRESS	TELEPHONE NUMBER	FAX	EMAIL	WEBSITE
Colorado	Consumer Protection Division, 1525 Sherman Street, 5th Floor, Denver, CO 80203-1760	303-866-5079	303-866-5443	n/a	n/a
Connecticut	Department of Consumer Protection, 165 Capitol Avenue, Hartford, CT 06106	860-713-6050	860-713-7243	n/a	www.ct.gov/dcp/
Delaware	Fraud and Consumer Protection Division, 820 N. French Street, Wilmington, DE 19801	302-577-8600	302-577-2496	attorney.general@state.de.us	www.state.de.us/attgen/
District of Columbia	Department of Consumer & Regulatory Affairs, 941 North Capitol St. NE, Washington, DC 20002	202-442-4400	202-442-9445	dcra@dc.gov	dcra.dc.gov/
Florida	Economic Crimes Unit, PL-01 The Capitol, Tallahassee, FL 32399-1050	850-414-3600	850-488-4483	n/a	myfloridalega.com/
Georgia	Governor's Office of Consumer Affairs, 2 Martin Luther King Jr. Drive, Suite 356, Atlanta, GA 30334	404-656-3790	404-651-9018	n/a	www2.state.ga.us/gaoca/
Hawaii	Office of Consumer Protection, 235 South Beretania St., room 801, Honolulu, HI 96813-2419	808-586-2636	808-586-2640	n/a	www.hawaii.gov/dcca/ocp/

State	Address	Phone 1	Phone 2	Email	Website
Idaho	Consumer Protection Unit, 650 West State St., Boise, ID 83720-0010	208-334-2424	208-334-2830	n/a	www.state.id.us/ag/
Illinois	Consumer Fraud Bureau, 100 West Randolph, 12th Floor, Chicago, IL 60601	312-814-3374	312-814-2593	ag_consumer@atg.state.il.us	www.illinoisattorneygeneral.gov/
Indiana	Consumer Protection Division, 302 West Washington St., Indianapolis, IN 46204	317-232-6201	317-232-7979	n/a	www.in.gov/attorneygeneral/
Iowa	Consumer Protection Division, 1305 East Walnut St., 2nd Floor, Des Moines, IA 50319	515-281-5926	515-281-6771	consumer@ag.state.ia.us	www.iowaattorneygeneral.org/
Kansas	Consumer Protection Division, 120 SW 10th, 2nd Floor, Topeka, KS 66612-1597	785-296-3751	785-291-3699	cprotect@ksag.org	www.ksag.org
Kentucky	Office of Consumer Protection Division, 1024 Capital Center Dr., Suite 200, Frankfort, KY 40601	502-696-5389	502-573-8317	attorney.general@ag.ky.gov	www.ag.ky.gov
Louisiana	Consumer Protection Division, P.O. Box 94005, Baton Rouge@@LA 70804-9005	1-800-351-4889	225-326-6499	n/a	www.ag.state.la.us/
Maine	Consumer Protection Division, 6 State House Station, Augusta, ME 04333	207-626-8800	207-626-8812	consumer.mediation@state.me.us	www.maine.gov/

STATE	ADDRESS	TELEPHONE NUMBER	FAX	EMAIL	WEBSITE
Maryland	Consumer Protection Division, Office of the Attorney General, 200 Saint Paul Place, 16th Floor, Baltimore, MD 21202-2021	410-576-6550	410-576-7040	consumer@oag.state.md.us	www.oag.state.md.us/consumer/
Massachusetts	Consumer Protection Division, One Ashburton Place, Boston, MA 02108	617-727-8400	617-727-3265	n/a	www.mass.gov/ago/
Michigan	Consumer Protection Division, P.O. Box 30213, Lansing, MI 48909	517-373-1140	517-241-3771	n/a	www.michigan.gov/ag/
Minnesota	Consumer Services Division, 445 Minnesota St., St. Paul, MN 55101	651-296-3353	651-282-2155	attorney.general@state.mn.us	www.ag.state.mn.us/consumer/
Mississippi	Consumer Protection Division, P.O. Box 22947, Jackson, MS 39225-2947	601-359-4230	601-359-4231	n/a	www.ago.state.ms.us/
Missouri	Consumer Protection Division, 207 W. High St.@@Jefferson City@@MO 65102	573-751-3321	573-751-0774	attgenmail@moago.org	www.ago.mo.gov/
Montana	Office of Consumer Protection, 1219 8th Ave., Helena, MT 59620-0151	406-444-4500	406-444-9680	n/a	www.mt.gov/consumer/

Nebraska	Office of the Attorney General, 2115 State Capitol, Lincoln, NE 68509	402-471-2682	402-471-0006	n/a	www.ago.state.ne.us/
Nevada	Consumer Affairs Division, 1850 East Sahara Ave., Suite 101, Las Vegas, NV 89104	702-486-7355	702-486-7371	ncad@fyiconsumer.org	www.fyiconsumer.org
New Hampshire	Consumer Protection Bureau, 33 Capitol St., Concord, NH 03301	603-271-3641	603-223-6202	n/a	www.doj.nh.gov/consumer/index.html
New Jersey	Division of Consumer Affairs, P. O. Box 45027, Newark, NJ 07101	973-504-6200	973-648-3538	askconsumeraffairs@lps.state.nj.us	www.state.nj.us/lps/ca/home.htm/
New Mexico	Consumer Protection Division, 407 Galisteo, Santa Fe, NM 87504-1508	505-827-6060	505-827-6685	n/a	www.ago.state.nm.us/
New York	Consumer Protection Board, 5 Empire State Plaza@@Suite 2102@@Albany@@NY 12223-1556	518-474-8583	518-474-2474	webmaster@consumer.state.ny.us	www.nysconsumer.gov/
North Carolina	Consumer Protection Division, 9001 Mail Service Center, Raleigh, NC 27699-9001	919-716-6000	919-716-6050	n/a	www.ncdoj.com/
North Dakota	Consumer Protection Division, 600 E. Boulevard Ave., Dept. 125, Bismarck, ND 58505	701-328-3404	n/a	cpat@state.nd.us	www.ag.state.nd.us/

DIRECTORY OF STATE CONSUMER PROTECTION AGENCIES

STATE	ADDRESS	TELEPHONE NUMBER	FAX	EMAIL	WEBSITE
Oklahoma	Consumer Protection Unit, 313 NE 21st Street, Oklahoma City, OK 73105	405-521-2029	405-528-1867	n/a	www.oag.state.ok.us/
Oregon	Consumer Protection Section, 1162 Court St. NE, Salem, OR 97310	503-947-4333	503-378-5017	n/a	www.doj.state.or.us/
Pennsylvania	Bureau of Consumer Protection, Strawberry Square, 16th Floor, Harrisburg, PA 17120	717-787-3391	717-787-8242	n/a	www.attorneygeneral.gov/
Rhode Island	Consumer Protection Unit, 150 South Main St., Providence, RI 02903	401-274-4400	401-222-5110	n/a	www.riag.state.ri.us/
South Carolina	Department of Consumer Affairs, 3600 Forest Drive, Suite 300, Columbia, SC 29250-5757	803-734-4200	803-734-4286	scdca@dca.state.sc.us	www.scconsumer.gov/
South Dakota	Consumer Affairs, 1302 E. Hwy 14, Suite 3, Pierre, SD 57501-8503	605-773-4400	605-773-7163	consumerhelp@state.sd.us	www.state.sd.us/atg/
Tennessee	Division of Consumer Affairs, 500 James Robertson Parkway, 5th Floor, Nashville, TN 37243-0600	615-741-4737	615-532-4994	consumer.affairs@state.tn.us	www.state.tn.us/consumer/

State	Address				
Texas	Consumer Protection Division, P.O. Box 12548, Austin, TX 78711-2548	512-463-2100	512-473-8301	cac@oag.state.tx.us	www.oag.state.tx.us/
Utah	Division of Consumer Protection, 160 East 300 South, Salt Lake City, UT 84114-6704	801-530-6601	801-530-6001	consumerprotection@utah.gov	www.consumerprotection.utah.gov/
Vermont	Consumer Assistance Program, 104 Morrill Hall, UVM, Burlington, VT 05405	802-656-3183	802-656-1423	consumer@uvm.edu	www.atg.state.vt.us/
Virginia	Consumer Litigation Section, 900 East Main St., Richmond, VA 23219	804-786-2116	804-786-0122	mail@oag.state.va.us	www.oag.state.va.us/
Washington	Regional Consumer Resource Center, 1125 Washington St. SE, Olympia, WA 98504-0100	1-800-551-4636	n/a	n/a	www.atg.wa.gov/
West Virginia	Consumer Protection Division, 812 Quarrier Street, 6th Floor, Charleston, WV 25326-1789	304-558-8986	304-558-0184	consumer@wvago.gov	www.wvago.us/
Wisconsin	Department of Consumer Protection, 2811 Agriculture Drive, Madison, WI 53708-8911	608-224-4949	608-224-4939	hotline@datcp.state.wi.us	www.datcp.state.wi.us/
Wyoming	Consumer Protection Unit, 123 State Capitol, 200 W. 24th Street, Cheyenne, WY 82002	307-777-7841	307-777-6869	agwebmaster@state.wy.us	attorneygeneral.state.wy.us/

SOURCE: The Federal Citizen Information Center of the U.S. General Services Administration

APPENDIX 3:
STATE STATUTES GOVERNING UNFAIR OR DECEPTIVE ACTS OR PRACTICES

STATE	STATUTE	COMMENTS
Alabama	Ala Code § 8-19-1	Prohibits unconscionable or deceptive practices including 21 enumerated practices. Violations must be knowing.
Alaska	Alaska Stat. § 45.50.471	Prohibits unfair methods of competition and unfair or deceptive acts and practices including 28 enumerated practices.
Arizona	Ariz. Rev. Stat. Ann. § 44-1521	Prohibits deceptive practices and omissions of material fact with intent.
Arkansas	Ark. Stat. Ann § 4-88-101	Prohibits deceptive practices including 7 enumerated practices, and omissions of material fact with intent to cause reliance.
California	Cal. Civ. Code § 1750	Prohibits unfair methods of competition and unfair or deceptive practices including 22 enumerated practices. Violation must be intentional.
Colorado	Colo. Rev. Stat. § 6-1-101	Prohibits deceptive practices including 30 enumerated practices.
Connecticut	Conn. Gen. Stat. § 42-110a	Prohibits unfair methods of competition and unfair or deceptive acts or practices.

STATE	STATUTE	COMMENTS
Delaware	Del. Code Ann. Tit. 6 § 2511 and § 2531	Prohibits deceptive practices or omissions of material fact with intent to cause reliance including 11 enumerated practices, and other conduct creating a likelihood of misunderstanding.
District of Columbia	D.C. Code Ann. § 28-3901	Prohibits deceptive, unfair or unlawful trade practices including 26 enumerated practices, and unconscionable terms.
Florida	Fla. Stat. Ann. § 501.201	Prohibits unfair methods of competition and unfair or deceptive acts or practices.
Georgia	Ga. Code Ann. § 10-1-370 and § 10-1-390	Prohibits deceptive practices and conduct likely to create misunderstanding including 11 enumerated practices, and unfair or deceptive acts or practices in consumer transactions or office supply transactions.
Hawaii	Haw. Rev. Stat. § 480 and § 481A	Prohibits unfair methods of competition and unfair or deceptive trade practices including 11 enumerated deceptive practices, and conduct creating misunderstanding.
Idaho	Idaho Code § 48-601	Prohibits unfair methods of competition and unfair or deceptive acts or practices including 16 enumerated practices, and prohibits misleading consumer practice and any unconscionable practice. Violators must know or should know about violation.
Illinois	Ill. Rev. Stat. Ch. 121 1/2 § 261 and § 311	Prohibits unfair methods of competition and unfair or deceptive acts or practices including concealment or omission of any material fact with the intent to cause reliance including 15 enumerated prohibitions, and 11 enumerated deceptive trade practices and other conduct likely to cause confusion.
Indiana	Ind. Code Ann. § 24-5-0.5-1	Prohibits numerous enumerated deceptive acts concerning consumer transactions including transactions involving contracts with unconscionable clauses.

    Consumer Rights Law

Iowa	Iowa Code Ann. § 714.16	Prohibits unfair or deceptive acts including 4 enumerated practices, or concealment, suppression or omissions of material fact with intent to cause reliance.
Kansas	Kan. Stat. Ann. § 50-623	Prohibits any deceptive acts or practices or omissions as to a material fact including 10 enumerated prohibitions, and unconscionable practices including 7 enumerated prohibitions concerning consumer transactions, and seller must know or have reason to know of violation of deceptive practice.
Kentucky	Ky. Rev. Stat. § 367.110	Prohibits unfair or deceptive acts or practices where unfair is construed to mean unconscionable.
Louisiana	La. Rev. Stat. Ann. § 51:1401	Prohibits unfair methods of competition and unfair or deceptive acts or practices.
Maine	Me. Rev. Stat. Ann. Tit. 5 § 206 and Tit. 10 § 1211	Prohibits unfair methods of competition and unfair or deceptive acts or practices including 11 enumerated deceptive practices and prohibition of conduct likely to create confusion or misunderstanding.
Maryland	Md. Com. Law Code Ann. § 13-101	Prohibits numerous enumerated unfair or deceptive trade practices.
Massachusetts	Mass. Gen. Laws Ann. Ch. 93A	Prohibits unfair methods of competition and unfair or deceptive acts or practices.
Michigan	Mich. Comp. Laws Ann. § 445.901	Prohibits unfair, unconscionable or deceptive practices including 29 enumerated practices.
Minnesota	Minn. Stat. Ann. §§ 8.31, § 325D.44, § 325F.67, and § 325F.69	Prohibits unfair, discriminatory and other unlawful practices including 13 enumerated deceptive practices, conduct which simultaneously creates a likelihood of confusion or misunderstanding, untrue deceptive or misleading advertising, and fraud misrepresentation and misleading statements.
Mississippi	Miss. Code Ann. § 75-24-1	Prohibits unfair methods of competition and unfair or deceptive acts or practices including 11 enumerated practices.

STATE	STATUTE	COMMENTS
Missouri	Mo. Rev. Stat. § 407.010	Prohibits deceptive acts or concealment or omissions of material fact with intent to cause reliance.
Montana	Mont. Code Ann. § 30-14-101	Prohibits unfair methods of competition and unfair or deceptive acts or practices.
Nebraska	Neb. Rev. Stat. § 59-1601 and § 87-302	Prohibits unfair methods of competition and unfair or deceptive acts or practices including 14 enumerated practices and all unconscionable acts by suppliers in consumer transactions.
Nevada	Nev. Rev. Stat. § 41.600 and § 598.360	Prohibits 17 enumerated deceptive trade practices.
New Hampshire	N.H. Rev. Stat. Ann. § 358-A:1	Prohibits unfair methods of competition and unfair or deceptive acts or practices including 12 enumerated prohibitions.
New Jersey	N.J. Stat. Ann. § 56:8-1	Prohibits unconscionable commercial practice, deception, fraud or knowing concealment, and suppression or omission of material fact with intent to cause reliance including numerous enumerated prohibitions.
New Mexico	N.M. Stat. Ann. § 57-12-1	Prohibits unfair or deceptive trade practices including 17 enumerated prohibitions and 2 enumerated unconscionable trade practices.
New York	N.Y. Exec. Law § 63(12) and N.Y. Gen. Bus. Law § 349 and § 350	Prohibits repeated fraudulent or illegal acts including deception, suppression or unconscionable contractual provisions, and deceptive acts or practices including false advertising.
North Carolina	N.C. Gen. Stat. § 75-1.1	Prohibits unfair methods of competition and unfair or deceptive acts or practices.
North Dakota	N.D. Gen. Stat. § 51-15-01	Prohibits deceptive practices with intent to cause reliance.

Ohio	Ohio Rev. Code Ann. § 1345.01 and § 4165	Prohibits unfair and deceptive acts or practices including 11 enumerated practices, and any unconscionable acts or practices including 7 enumerated examples.
Oklahoma	Okla. Stat. Ann. Tit. 15 § 751 and Tit. 78 § 51	Prohibits 17 enumerated unlawful practices and 11 enumerated deceptive trade practices.
Oregon	Or. Rev. Stat. § 646.605	Prohibits 2 enumerated unconscionable tactics and 20 enumerated unfair or deceptive acts or practices including any violation of attorney general UDAP rules.
Pennsylvania	Pa. Stat. Ann. Tit. 73 § 201-1	Prohibits 15 enumerated unfair methods of competition and unfair or deceptive acts or practices and any other conduct likely to create confusion.
Rhode Island	R.I. Gen. Law § 6-13.1-1	Prohibits 17 enumerated unfair methods of competition and unfair or deceptive practices.
South Carolina	S.C. Code Ann. § 39-5-10	Prohibits unfair methods of competition and unfair or deceptive acts or practices.
South Dakota	S.D. Codified Laws Ann. § 37-24-1	Prohibits deceptive acts or practices including 14 enumerated prohibitions.
Tennessee	Tenn. Code Ann. § 47-18-101	Prohibits unfair or deceptive acts or practices including 20 enumerated prohibitions and any other deceptive consumer act.
Texas	Tex. Bus. & Com. Code Ann. § 17.41	Prohibits deceptive acts or practices including 23 enumerated prohibitions.
Utah	Utah Code Ann. §§ 13-2-1, 13-5-1, and 13-11-1	Prohibits unfair methods of competition including many enumerated unlawful practices and prohibits deceptive acts or practices by a supplier in consumer transactions including 14 enumerated prohibitions and unconscionable practices by suppliers in consumer transactions.

STATE	STATUTE	COMMENTS
Vermont	Vt. Stat. Ann. Tit. 9 § 2451	Prohibits unfair methods of competition and unfair or deceptive acts or practices.
Virginia	Va. Code § 59.1-196	Prohibits 24 enumerated fraudulent acts.
Washington	Wash. Rev. Code Ann. § 19.86.010	Prohibits unfair methods of competition and unfair or deceptive acts. Violations must be injurious to the public interest.
West Virginia	W. Va. Code § 46A-6-101	Prohibits unfair methods of competition and unfair or deceptive acts or practices.
Wisconsin	Wis. Stat. Ann. § 100.18 and § 100.20	Prohibits untrue, deceptive or misleading representations including 14 itemized deceptive representations, and unfair methods of competition and unfair trade practices.
Wyoming	Wyo. Stat. § 40-12-101	Prohibits enumerated practices plus other unfair or deceptive acts or practices. Violations must be knowing.

APPENDIX 4:
THE FTC MAIL OR TELEPHONE ORDER MERCHANDISE RULE – SELECTED PROVISIONS

SECTION 435.1 - THE RULE

In connection with mail or telephone-order sales in or affecting commerce, as "commerce" is defined in the Federal Trade Commission Act, it constitutes an unfair method of competition, and an unfair or deceptive act or practice for a seller:

(a) 1. To solicit any order for the sale of merchandise to be ordered by the buyer through the mails or by telephone unless, at the time of the solicitation, the seller has a reasonable basis to expect that it will be able to ship any ordered merchandise to the buyer:

i. Within that time clearly and conspicuously stated in any such solicitation, or

ii. if no time is clearly and conspicuously stated, within thirty (30) days after receipt of a properly completed order from the buyer. Provided, however, Where, at the time the merchandise is ordered the buyer applies to the seller for credit to pay for the merchandise in whole or in part, the seller shall have 50 days, rather than 30 days, to perform the actions required in § 435.1 (a)(1)(ii) of this part.

2. To provide any buyer with any revised shipping date, as provided in paragraph (b) of this section, unless, at the time any such revised shipping date is provided, the seller has a reasonable basis for making such representation regarding a definite revised shipping date.

3. To inform any buyer that it is unable to make any representation regarding the length of any delay unless:

i. the seller has a reasonable basis for so informing the buyer and

ii. the seller informs the buyer of the reason or reasons for the delay.

4. In any action brought by the Federal Trade Commission alleging a violation of this part, the failure of a respondent-seller to have records or other documentary proof establishing its use of systems and procedures which assure the shipment of merchandise in the ordinary course of business within any applicable time set forth in this part will create a rebuttable presumption that the seller lacked a reasonable basis for any expectation of shipment within said applicable time.

(b) 1. Where a seller is unable to ship merchandise within the applicable time set forth in paragraph (a)(1) of this section, to fail to offer to the buyer, clearly and conspicuously and without prior demand, an option either to consent to a delay in shipping or to cancel the buyer's order and receive a prompt refund. Said offer shall be made within a reasonable time after the seller first becomes aware of its inability to ship within the applicable time set forth in paragraph (a)(1) of this section, but in no event later than said applicable time.

i. Any offer to the buyer of such an option shall fully inform the buyer regarding the buyer's right to cancel the order and to obtain a prompt refund and shall provide a definite revised shipping date, but where the seller lacks a reasonable basis for providing a definite revised shipping date the notice shall inform the buyer that the seller is unable to make any representation regarding the length of the delay.

ii. Where the seller has provided a definite revised shipping date which is thirty (30) days or less later than the applicable time set forth in paragraph (a)(1) of this section, the offer of said option shall expressly inform the buyer that, unless the seller receives, prior to shipment and prior to the expiration of the definite revised shipping date, a response from the buyer rejecting the delay and cancelling the order, the buyer will be deemed to have consented to a delayed shipment on or before the definite revised shipping date.

iii. Where the seller has provided a definite revised shipping date which is more than thirty (30) days later than the applicable time set forth in paragraph (a)(1) of this section or where the seller is unable to provide a definite revised shipping date and therefore informs the buyer that it is unable to make any representation regarding the length of the delay, the offer of said option shall also expressly inform the buyer that the buyer's order will automatically be deemed to have been cancelled unless:

A. the seller has shipped the merchandise within thirty (30) days of the applicable time set forth in paragraph (a)(1) of this section, and has received no cancellation prior to shipment, or

B. the seller has received from the buyer within thirty (30) days of said applicable time, a response specifically consenting to said shipping delay. Where the seller informs the buyer that it is unable to make any representation regarding the length of the delay, the buyer shall be expressly informed that, should the buyer consent to an indefinite delay, the buyer will have a continuing right to cancel the buyer's order at any time after the applicable time set forth in paragraph (a)(1) of this section by so notifying the seller prior to actual shipment.

iv. Nothing in this paragraph shall prohibit a seller who furnishes a definite revised shipping date pursuant to paragraph (b)(1)(i) of this section, from requesting, simultaneously with or at any time subsequent to the offer of an option pursuant to paragraph (b)(1) of this section, the buyer's express consent to a further unanticipated delay beyond the definite revised shipping date in the form of a response from the buyer specifically consenting to said further delay. Provided, however, That where the seller solicits consent to an unanticipated indefinite delay the solicitation shall expressly inform the buyer that, should the buyer so consent to an indefinite delay, the buyer shall have a continuing right to cancel the buyer's order at any time after the definite revised shipping date by so notifying the seller prior to actual shipment.

2. Where a seller is unable to ship merchandise on or before the definite revised shipping date provided under paragraph (b)(1)(i) of this section and consented to by the buyer pursuant to paragraph (b)(1)(ii) or (iii) of this section, to fail to offer to the buyer, clearly and conspicuously and without prior demand, a renewed option either to consent to a further delay or to cancel the order and to receive a prompt refund. Said offer shall be made within a reasonable time after the seller first becomes aware of its inability to ship before the said definite revised date, but in no event later than the expiration of the definite revised shipping date:

Provided, however, That where the seller previously has obtained the buyer's express consent to an unanticipated delay until a specific date beyond the definite revised shipping date, pursuant to paragraph (b)(1)(iv) of this section or to a further delay until a specific date beyond the definite revised shipping date pursuant to paragraph (b)(2) of this section, that date to which the buyer has expressly consented shall supersede the definite revised shipping date for purposes of paragraph (b)(2) of this section.

i. Any offer to the buyer of said renewed option shall provide the buyer with a new definite revised shipping date, but where the seller lacks a reasonable basis for providing a new definite revised shipping date, the notice shall inform the buyer that the seller is unable to make any representation regarding the length of the further delay.

ii. The offer of a renewed option shall expressly inform the buyer that, unless the seller receives, prior to the expiration of the old definite revised shipping date or any date superseding the old definite revised shipping date, notification from the buyer specifically consenting to the further delay, the buyer will be deemed to have rejected any further delay, and to have cancelled the order if the seller is in fact unable to ship prior to the expiration of the old definite revised shipping date or any date superseding the old definite revised shipping date.

Provided, however, That where the seller offers the buyer the option to consent to an indefinite delay the offer shall expressly inform the buyer that, should the buyer so consent to an indefinite delay, the buyer shall have a continuing right to cancel the buyer's order at any time after the old definite revised shipping date or any date superseding the old definite revised shipping date.

iii. Paragraph (b)(2) of this section shall not apply to any situation where a seller, pursuant to the provisions of paragraph (b)(1)(iv) of this section, has previously obtained consent from the buyer to an indefinite extension beyond the first revised shipping date.

3. Wherever a buyer has the right to exercise any option under this part or to cancel an order by so notifying the seller prior to shipment, to fail to furnish the buyer with adequate means, at the seller's expense, to exercise such option or to notify the seller regarding cancellation.

Nothing in paragraph (b) of this section shall prevent a seller, where it is unable to make shipment within the time set forth in paragraph (a)(1) of this section or within a delay period consented to by the buyer, from deciding to consider the order cancelled and providing the buyer with notice of said decision within a reasonable time after it becomes aware of said inability to ship, together with a prompt refund.

(c) To fail to deem an order cancelled and to make a prompt refund to the buyer whenever:

1. The seller receives, prior to the time of shipment, notification from the buyer cancelling the order pursuant to any option, renewed option or continuing option under this part;

2. The seller has, pursuant to paragraph (b)(1)(iii) of this section, provided the buyer with a definite revised shipping date which is more than thirty (30) days later than the applicable time set forth in paragraph (a)(1) of this section or has notified the buyer that it is unable to make any representation regarding the length of the delay and the seller:

    i. has not shipped the merchandise within thirty (30) days of the applicable time set forth in paragraph (a)(1) of this section, and

    ii. has not received the buyer's express consent to said shipping delay within said thirty (30) days;

3. The seller is unable to ship within the applicable time set forth in paragraph (b)(2) of this section, and has not received, within the said applicable time, the buyer's consent to any further delay;

4. The seller has notified the buyer of its inability to make shipment and has indicated its decision not to ship the merchandise;

5. The seller fails to offer the option prescribed in paragraph (b)(1) of this section and has not shipped the merchandise within the applicable time set forth in paragraph (a)(1) of this section.

In any action brought by the Federal Trade Commission, alleging a violation of this part, the failure of a respondent-seller to have records or other documentary proof establishing its use of systems and procedures which assure compliance, in the ordinary course of business, with any requirement of paragraph (b) or (c) of this section will create a rebuttable presumption that the seller failed to comply with said requirement.

* * *

SECTION 435.3 – LIMITED APPLICABILITY

(a) This part shall not apply to:

1. Subscriptions, such as magazine sales, ordered for serial delivery, after the initial shipment is made in compliance with this part.

2. Orders of seeds and growing plants.

3. Orders made on a collect-on-delivery (C.O.D.) basis.

4. Transactions governed by the Federal Trade Commission's Trade Regulation Rule entitled "Use of Negative Option Plans by Sellers in Commerce," 16 CFR Part 425.

(b) By taking action in this area:

1. The Federal Trade Commission does not intend to preempt action in the same area, which is not inconsistent with this part, by any State, municipal, or other local government. This part does not annul or diminish any rights or remedies provided to consumers by any State law, municipal ordinance, or other local regulation, insofar as those rights or remedies are equal to or greater than those provided by this part. In addition, this part does not supersede those provisions of any State law, municipal ordinance, or other local regulation which impose obligations or liabilities upon sellers, when sellers subject to this part are not in compliance therewith.

2. This part does supersede those provisions of any State law, municipal ordinance, or other local regulation which are inconsistent with this part to the extent that those provisions do not provide a buyer with rights which are equal to or greater than those rights granted a buyer by this part. This part also supersedes those provisions of any State law, municipal ordinance, or other local regulation requiring that a buyer be notified of a right which is the same as a right provided by this part but requiring that a buyer be given notice of this right in a language, form, or manner which is different in any way from that required by this part. In those instances where any State law, municipal ordinance, or other local regulation contains provisions, some but not all of which are partially or completely superseded by this part, the provisions or portions of those provisions which have not been superseded retain their full force and effect.

3. If any provision of this part, or its application to any person, partnership, corporation, act or practice is held invalid, the remainder of this part or the application of the provision to any other person, partnership, corporation, act or practice shall not be affected thereby.

APPENDIX 5:

DIRECTORY OF U.S. CONSUMER PRODUCT SAFETY COMMISSION REGIONAL OFFICES

OFFICE	ADDRESS	TELEPHONE	FAX	EMAIL	WEBSITE
National Headquarters	U.S. Consumer Product Safety Commission, 4330 East West Highway, Bethesda 20814	301-504-7923	301-504-0025	info@cpsc.gov	www.cpsc.gov/
Central Regional Office	230 S. Dearborn Street, Room 2944, Chicago, IL 60604-1601	312-353-8260	n/a	info@cpsc.gov	www.cpsc.gov/
Eastern Regional Office	201 Varick Street, Room 903, New York, NY 10014-4811	212-620-4120	n/a	info@cpsc.gov	www.cpsc.gov/
Western Regional Office	1301 Clay Street, Suite 610-N, Oakland, CA 94612	510-637-4050	n/a	info@cpsc.gov	www.cpsc.gov/
Consumer Hotline	Washington, DC 20207	1-800-638-2772	n/a	info@cpsc.gov	www.cpsc.gov/

APPENDIX 6:
DIRECTORY OF NATIONAL HIGHWAY TRAFFIC SAFETY ADMINISTRATION REGIONAL OFFICES

REGION	AREAS COVERED	ADDRESS	TELEPHONE	FAX	EMAIL	WEBSITE
NEW ENGLAND – REGION 1	CT, ME, MA, NH, RI, VT	Volpe National Transportation Systems Center, Kendall Square - Code 903, Cambridge, MA 02142	617-494-3427	617-494-3646	NewEnglandRegion@ dot.gov	http://www. nhtsa.dot.gov/ nhtsa/whatis/ regions/ Region01/ Index.html/
EASTERN REGION 2	NJ, NY, PR, VI	222 Mamaroneck Avenue, Suite 204, White Plains, NY 10605	914-682-6162	914-682-6239	EasternRegion@dot.gov	http://www. nhtsa.dot.gov/ nhtsa/whatis/ regions/ Region02/ Index.html/

REGION	AREAS COVERED	ADDRESS	TELEPHONE	FAX	EMAIL	WEBSITE
MIDATLANTIC REGION 3	DE, DC, MD, PA, VA, WV	10 South Howard Street, Suite 6700, Baltimore, MD 21201	410-962-0077	410-962-2770	MidAtlanticRegion@dot.gov	http://www.nhtsa.dot.gov/nhtsa/whatis/regions/Region03/Index.html/
SOUTHEAST REGION 4	AL, FL, GA, KY, MS, NC, SC, TN	61 Forsyth Street SW, Atlanta, GA 30303	404-562-3739	404-562-3763	SoutheastRegion@dot.gov	http://www.nhtsa.dot.gov/nhtsa/whatis/regions/Region04/Index.html/
GREAT LAKES REGION 5	IL, IN, MI, MN, OH, WI	19900 Governors Drive, Suite 201, Olympia Fields, IL 60461,	708-503-8822	708-503-8991	GreatLakesRegion@dot.gov	http://www.nhtsa.dot.gov/nhtsa/whatis/regions/Region05/Index.html/
SOUTH CENTRAL REGION 6	AR, LA, NM, OK, TX, Indian Nations	819 Taylor Street, Room 8A38, Fort Worth, TX 76102-6177	817-978-3653	817-978-8339	SouthCentralRegion@dot.gov	http://www.nhtsa.dot.gov/nhtsa/whatis/regions/Region06/Index.html/

CENTRAL REGION 7	IA, KS, MO, NE	901 Locust St., Room 466, Kansas City, MO 64106	816-329-3900	816-329-3910	CentralRegion@ dot.gov	http://www. nhtsa.dot.gov/ nhtsa/whatis/ regions/ Region07/ Index.html
ROCKY MOUNTAIN REGION 8	CO, MT, ND, SD, UT, WY	12300 West Dakota Avenue, Suite 140, Lakewood, CO 80228	720-963-3100	720-963-3124	RockyMountainRegion@ dot.gov	http://www. nhtsa.dot.gov/ nhtsa/whatis/ regions/ Region08/ Index.html/
WESTERN REGION 9	American Samoa, AZ, CA, Guam, HI, N. Marianas, NV	201 Mission Street, Suite 2250, San Francisco, CA 94105	415-744-3089	415-744-2532	WesternRegion@ dot.gov	http://www. nhtsa.dot.gov/ nhtsa/whatis/ regions/ Region09/ Index.html
PACIFIC NORTHWEST REGION 10	AK, ID, OR, WA	915 Second Avenue, Seattle, WA 98174	206-220-7640	206-220-7651	PacificNorthwestRegion@ dot.gov	http://www. nhtsa.dot.gov/ nhtsa/whatis/ regions/ Region10/ Index.html/

SOURCE: National Highway Traffic Safety Administration

APPENDIX 7:
DIRECTORY OF U.S. FOOD AND DRUG ADMINISTRATION REGIONAL OFFICES

REGION	ADDRESS	TELEPHONE	FAX
HEADQUARTERS	5600 Fishers Lane, Rockville, MD 20857	1-888-463-6332	n/a
NORTHEAST REGION	158-15 Liberty Avenue, Jamaica, NY 11434	718-662-5416	718-662-5434
CENTRAL REGION	900 U.S. Customhouse, 200 Chestnut Street, Philadelphia, PA 19106	215-597-4390	215-597-5798
SOUTHEAST REGION	60 Eight Street NE, Atlanta, GA 30309	404-253-1171	404-253-1207
SOUTHWEST REGION	4040 North Central Expressway, Suite 900, Dallas, TX 75204	214-253-4904	214-253-4965
PACIFIC REGION	1301 Clay Street, Oakland, CA 94612-5217	510-637-3960	510-637-3976

SOURCE: U.S. Food and Drug Administration

APPENDIX 8:
DIRECTORY OF U.S. ENVIRONMENTAL PROTECTION AGENCY REGIONAL OFFICES

REGION	AREAS COVERED	ADDRESS	TELEPHONE	FAX	WEBSITE
HEADQUARTERS	Nationwide	1200 Pennsylvania Avenue NW, Washington, DC 20460	202-272-0167	n/a	www.epa.gov/
REGION 1	CT, MA, ME, NH, RI, VT	1 Congress Street, Boston, MA 02114-2023	617-918-1111	617-918-1809	www.epa.gov/region1/
REGION 2	NJ, NY, PR, VI	290 Broadway, New York, NY 10007-1866	212-637-3660	212-637-3526	www.epa.gov/region2/
REGION 3	DC, DE, MD, PA,VA,WV	1650 Arch Street, Philadelphia, PA 19103-2029	215-814-5000	215-814-5103	www.epa.gov/region3/
REGION 4	AL, FL, GA, KY, MS,NC, SC, TN	61 Forsyth Street, Atlanta, GA 30303-8960	404-562-9900	404-562-8174	www.epa.gov/region4/
REGION 5	IL, IN, MI, MN, OH, WI	77 West Jackson Boulevard, Chicago, IL 60604-3507	312-353-2000	312-353-4135	www.epa.gov/region5/

REGION	AREAS COVERED	ADDRESS	TELEPHONE	FAX	WEBSITE
REGION 6	AR, LA, NM,OK, TX	1445 Ross Avenue, Suite 1200, Dallas, TX 75202-2733	214-665-2200	214-665-7113	www.epa.gov/region6/
REGION 7	IA, KS, MO, NE	901 North 5th Street, Kansas City, KS 66101	913-551-7003	n/a	www.epa.gov/region7/
REGION 8	CO, MT, ND, SD, UT, WY	1595 Wynkoop Street, Denver, CO 80202-1129	303-312-6312	303-312-6339	www.epa.gov/region8/
REGION 9	AZ, CA, HI, NV	75 Hawthorne Street, San Francisco, CA 94105	415-947-8000	415-947-3553	www.epa.gov/region9/
REGION 10	AK, ID, OR, WA	1200 Sixth Avenue, Seattle, WA 98101	206-553-1200	n/a	www.epa.gov/region10/

SOURCE: U.S. Environmental Protection Agency

APPENDIX 9:
TABLE OF STATE USURY LAWS

STATE	LEGAL RATE	USURY LIMIT
ALABAMA	6%	8%
ALASKA	10.5%	more than 5% above the Federal Reserve interest rate on the day the loan was made
ARIZONA	10%	n/a
ARKANSAS	6%	for non-consumers the usury limit is 5% above the Federal Reserve's interest rate; for consumers the general usury limit is 17%
CALIFORNIA	10% for consumers	for non-consumers the usury limit is more than 5% greater than the rate of the Federal Reserve Bank of San Francisco
COLORADO	8%	45% (general); 12% (consumers)
CONNECTICUT	8%	12%
DELAWARE	5% over the Federal Reserve rate	n/a
DISTRICT OF COLUMBIA	6%	24%
FLORIDA	12%	18% (25% on loans above $500,000)
GEORGIA	7%	16% (loans below $3,000); 5% (loans above $3,000)
HAWAII	10%	12% (consumer transactions)
IDAHO	12%	n/a
ILLINOIS	5%	9%
INDIANA	10%	n/a

STATE	LEGAL RATE	USURY LIMIT
IOWA	10%	12% (consumer transactions)
KANSAS	10%	15% (general); 18% (consumer transactions-first $1,000); 14.45% (above $1,000)
KENTUCKY	8%	4% greater than the Federal Reserve rate or 19%, whichever is greater; no limit (loans above $15,000)
LOUISIANA	one point over the average prime rate, not to exceed 14% nor be less than 7%	12% (individuals); no limit (corporations)
MAINE	6%	n/a
MARYLAND	6%	24%
MASSACHUSETTS	6%	20% (general)
MICHIGAN	5%	7% (general)
MINNESOTA	6%	8%
MISSISSIPPI	9%	more than 10% or more than 5% above federal reserve rate; no limit (commercial loans above $5,000)
MISSOURI	9%	no usury defense for corporations
MONTANA	10%	above 6% greater than NYC bank prime rate
NEBRASKA	6%	16% (general)
NEVADA	12%	no usury limit
NEW HAMPSHIRE	10%	no usury limit
NEW JERSEY	6%	30% (individuals); 50% (corporations)
NEW MEXICO	15%	n/a
NEW YORK	9%	16% (general)
NORTH CAROLINA	8%	8% (general)
NORTH DAKOTA	6%	5-1/2% above the six-month treasury bill interest rate

STATE	LEGAL RATE	USURY LIMIT
OKLAHOMA	6%	10% (unless person is licensed to make consumer loans); 45% (non-consumer loans)
OREGON	9%	12% (loans below $50,000 5% above discount rate (commercial paper)
PENNSYLVANIA	6%	6% (general for loans below $50,000 except loans with a lien on non-residential real estate; loans to corporations; loans that have no collateral above $35,000
PUERTO RICO	6%	as set by Finance Board of Office of Commissioner of Financial Institutions
RHODE ISLAND	12%	21% (general); 9% (T-Bills)
SOUTH CAROLINA	8.75%	no usury limit subject to federal criminal laws against loan sharking
SOUTH DAKOTA	15%	no usury limit
TENNESSEE	10%	24% or four points above average prime loan rate whichever is less
TEXAS	6%	n/a
UTAH	10%	floating rates (consumer transactions)
VERMONT	12%	12% (general); 18% (retail installment contracts-first $500); 15% (retail installment contracts-above $500)
VIRGINIA	8%	multiple regulated rates (consumer loans); no usury limit (corporations and business loans); exempt (loans over $5,000 for business or investment purposes)
WASHINGTON	12%	12% (general) the legal rate is 12% or four points above the average T-Bill rate for the past 26 weeks whichever is greater
WEST VIRGINIA	6%	8% (contractual rate); Commissioner of Banking issues rates (real estate loans)
WISCONSIN	5%	no general usury limit (corporations); the legal rate of interest is 5%
WYOMING	10%	n/a

APPENDIX 10:
NOTIFICATION LETTER TO CREDIT REPORTING AGENCY – ERRONEOUS INFORMATION DISPUTE

[Date]

[Name of Credit Reporting Agency]
[Address]
[City, State, Zip Code]

Attn: Complaint Department

Dear Sir or Madam:

I am writing to dispute the following information contained in my credit file with your Company. The items I dispute are also encircled on the attached copy of the credit report I received from your office, as follows:

Item #1: [Identify item(s) disputed by name of source, such as creditors or tax court, and identify type of item, such as credit account, judgment, etc.] This item is [inaccurate or incomplete] because [describe what is inaccurate or incomplete and why]. I am requesting that the item be deleted [or request another specific change[to correct the information. Enclosed are copies of [use this sentence if applicable and describe any enclosed documentation, such as payment records, court documents] supporting my position.

Item #2: Same as above for any additional disputed information.

Please reinvestigate [this/these) matter(s) and [delete or correct] the disputed item(s) as soon as possible.

Sincerely,

John Doe

Enclosures: [List what you are enclosing]

APPENDIX 11:
ANNUAL CREDIT REPORT
REQUEST FORM

EQUIFAX   **experian**   **TransUnion.**

Annual Credit Report Request Form

You have the right to get a free copy of your credit file disclosure, commonly called a credit report, once every 12 months, from each of the nationwide consumer credit reporting companies - Equifax, Experian and TransUnion.

For instant access to your free credit report, visit www.annualcreditreport.com.

For more information on obtaining your free credit report, visit www.annualcreditreport.com or call 877-322-8228.

Use this form if you prefer to write to request your credit report from any, or all, of the nationwide consumer credit reporting companies. The following information is required to process your request. **Omission of any information may delay your request.**

Once complete, fold (do not staple or tape), place into a #10 envelope, affix required postage and mail to:
Annual Credit Report Request Service P.O. Box 105281 Atlanta, GA 30348-5281.

Please use a Black or Blue Pen and write your responses in PRINTED CAPITAL LETTERS without touching the sides of the boxes like the examples listed below:

A B C D E F G H I J K L M N O P Q R S T U V W X Y Z   0 1 2 3 4 5 6 7 8 9

Social Security Number:

Date of Birth:

Month   Day   Year

- - - - - Fold Here - Fold Here - - - - -

First Name   M.I.

Last Name   JR, SR, III, etc.

Current Mailing Address:

House Number   Street Name

Apartment Number / Private Mailbox   For Puerto Rico Only: Print Urbanization Name

City   State   ZipCode

Previous Mailing Address (complete only if at current mailing address for less than two years):

House Number   Street Name

- - - - - Fold Here - Fold Here - - - - -

Apartment Number / Private Mailbox   For Puerto Rico Only: Print Urbanization Name

City   State   ZipCode

Shade Circle Like This → ●

Not Like This → ⊠ ⊘

I want a credit report from (shade each that you would like to receive):

○ Equifax
○ Experian
○ TransUnion

○ Shade here if, for security reasons, you want your credit report to include no more than the last four digits of your Social Security Number.

If additional information is needed to process your request, the consumer credit reporting company will contact you by mail.

Your request will be processed within 15 days of receipt and then mailed to you.

Copyright 2004, Central Source LLC

31238

APPENDIX 12:
TABLE OF STATE DEBT COLLECTION STATUTES

STATE	STATUTE
Alabama	Alabama Code §40-12-80
Alaska	Alaska Statutes §§8.24.0.011 et seq.
Arizona	Arizona Revised Statutes Annotated §§32-1001 et seq.
Arkansas	Arkansas Statutes Annotated §617-21-104 et seq.
California	California Civil Code §§1788 et seq.
Colorado	Colorado Revised Statutes §§5-10101 et seq; 12-14-101 et seq.
Connecticut	Connecticut General Statutes Annotated §§36-243. a et seq; 42-127 et seq.
Delaware	Delaware Code Annotated,, Title 30,, §2301(13).
District of Columbia	D.C. Code Annotated §§22-3423 et seq; 28-3814 et seq.
Florida	Florida Statutes §§559.55 et seq.
Georgia	Georgia Code Annotated §§7-3-1 et seq.
Hawaii	Hawaii Revised Statutes §§443-B-1 et seq.
Idaho	Idaho Code §§26-2222 et seq.
Illinois	Illinois Annotated Statutes,, Chapter 111,, §§2001 et seq.

STATE	STATUTE
Indiana	Indiana Code Annotated §§25-11-1-1 et seq.
Iowa	Iowa Code Annotated §§537.7101 et seq.
Kansas	Kansas Statutes Annotated §16a-5-107.
Kentucky	None.
Louisiana	Louisiana Revised Statutes Annotated §§9:3510 et seq.
Maine	Maine Revised Statutes Annotated,, Title 32 §§11,001 et seq; Title 9-A §§1.101 et seq.
Maryland	Maryland Annotated Code,, Article 56 §§323 et seq; Maryland Com. Law Code Annotated,, §§14-201 et seq.
Massachusetts	Massachusetts General Laws Annotated,, Chapter 93 §§24 et seq; §49.
Michigan	Michigan Compiled Laws Annotated §19.655; §18.425.
Minnesota	None.
Missouri	None.
Montana	None.
Nebraska	Nebraska Revised Statutes §§45-601 et seq; 45-175 et seq.
Nevada	Nevada Revised Statutes §§649.005 et seq.
New Hampshire	New Hampshire Revised Statutes Annotated §§358-C:1 et seq.
New Jersey	New Jersey Statutes Annotated §§45:18-1 et seq.
New Mexico	New Mexico Statutes Annotated §§61-18A-1 et seq.
New York	New York General Law §§600 et seq.
North Carolina	North Carolina General Statutes §§66-49.24 et seq; 75-50 et seq.
North Dakota	North Dakota Cent. Code §§13-05-01 et seq.
Ohio	None.

STATE	STATUTE
Oklahoma	None.
Oregon	Oregon Revised Statutes §§646.639 et seq; 697.010 et seq.
Pennsylvania	18 Pennsylvania Cons. Statutes Annotated §§7311; 201-1 et seq.
Rhode Island	None.
South Carolina	South Carolina Code Annotated §37-5-108.
South Dakota	None.
Tennessee	Tennessee Code Annotated §§62-20-101 et seq.
Texas	Texas Revised Civ. Statutes Annotated,, Arts. 5069-11.01 et seq.
Utah	Utah Code Annotated §§12-1-1 et seq.
Vermont	Vermont Statutes Annotated,, Title 9 §§2451a et seq.
Virginia	Virginia Code Annotated §§18.2 et seq.
Washington	Washington Revised Code Annotated §§19.16.100 et seq.
West Virginia	West Virginia Code §§47-16-1 §§18.2 et seq; 46A-2-101 et seq.
Wisconsin	Wisconsin Statutes Annotated §§218.04; 427.101 et seq.
Wyoming	Wyoming Statutes §§33-11-101 et seq.

APPENDIX 13:
NOTIFICATION LETTER TO CREDIT CARD ISSUER – BILLING ERROR

Date of Letter

By Certified Mail #
Return Receipt Requested

Name of Credit Card Issuer
Address
City, State, Zip Code
Attn: Billing Inquiries

Dear Sir or Madam:

I am writing to dispute a billing error in the amount of [state dollar amount] on my account. The amount is inaccurate because [describe the problem]. I am requesting that the error be corrected, that any finance and other charges related to the disputed amount be credited as well, and that I receive an accurate statement.

Enclosed are copies of [use this sentence to describe any enclosed information, such as sales slips, payment records] supporting my position. Please investigate this matter and correct the billing error as soon as possible.

Sincerely,

John Doe

Enclosures: [List what you are enclosing.]

APPENDIX 14:
DIRECTORY OF STATE LEMON LAW WEBSITES

STATE	WEBSITE
Alabama	http://www.ago.alabama.gov/alcode/law_lemon.htm
Alaska	http://www.law.state.ak.us/department/civil/consumer/cpindex.html
Arizona	http://www.azag.gov/consumer/index.html
Arkansas	http://www.ag.state.ar.us/consumer/lemonlaw.html
California	http://caag.state.ca.us/consumers/general/lemon.htm
Colorado	http://www.ago.state.co.us/consprot/lemonlaw/Lemonlaw.htm
Connecticut	http://www.ct.gov/dcp/site/default.asp
Delaware	http://www.ct.gov/dcp/site/default.asp
District of Columbia	http://occ.dc.gov/occ/cwp/view.asp?a=1223&q=531275
Florida	http://occ.dc.gov/occ/cwp/view.asp?a=1223&q=531275
Georgia	http://consumer.georgia.gov
Hawaii	http://www.hawaii.gov/dcca/areas/rico
Idaho	http://www2.state.id.us/ag/consumer/index.htm
Illinois	http://www.ag.state.il.us/consumers/index.html
Indiana	http://www.in.gov/attorneygeneral/consumer/lemonlaw.html
Iowa	http://www.state.ia.us/government/ag/consumer/advisories/lemonlawall020402.html

STATE	WEBSITE
Kansas	http://www.ksag.org/Publications/ConsumerCorner/Car/index.htm
Kentucky	http://www.law.state.ky.us/cp/cptips.htm#New%20Cars
Louisiana	http://ladoj.ag.state.la.us/publications/lemonlaw2.htm
Maine=	http://www.maine.gov/ag/index.php?r=protection&s=lemon_law&t
Maryland	http://www.oag.state.md.us/consumer/lemon.htm
Massachusetts	http://www.mass.gov/portal/site/massgovportal/menuitem.91646817bed931c14db4a11030468a0c/?pageID=ocasubtopic&L=4&sid=Eoca&L0=Home&L1=Consumer&L2=Autos&L3=Buying+and+Selling
Michigan	http://www.michigan.gov/ag/0,1607,7-164-17331-42077--,00.html
Minnesota	http://www.ag.state.mn.us/consumer/cars/MNCarlaws/MNCarLaws_1.htm
Mississippi	http://www.ago.state.ms.us/divisions/consumer/
Missouri	http://www.ago.state.mo.us/consumercomplaint.htm
Montana	http://www.discoveringmontana.com/doa/consumerprotection/lemonlaw.asp
Nebraska	http://www.dmv.state.ne.us/legal/lemon.html
Nevada	http://ag.state.nv.us/actionbutton/bcp/bcp.htm
New Hampshire	http://nh.gov/safety/dmv/lemonlaw/index.html
New Jersey	http://www.state.nj.us/lps/ca/brief/lemon.htm
New Mexico	http://www.ago.state.nm.us/divs/cons/cons_faqs_auto.htm
New York	http://www.oag.state.ny.us/consumer/cars/newcarlemon.html
North Carolina	http://www.jus.state.nc.us/cp/lemon.htm
North Dakota	http://www.ag.state.nd.us
Ohio	http://www.ag.state.oh.us/index.asp
Oklahoma	http://www.oag.state.ok.us/
Oregon	http://www.doj.state.or.us/lemonlaw.htm
Pennsylvania	http://www.attorneygeneral.gov/pei/know/lemonlaw.htm
Rhode Island	http://www.riag.state.ri.us/civil/index.php

STATE	WEBSITE
South Carolina	http://www.scconsumer.gov/
South Dakota	http://www.state.sd.us/attorney/office/divisions/consumer/default.asp
Tennessee	http://www.state.tn.us/consumer/lemon.html
Texas	http://www.dot.state.tx.us/mvd/lemon/lemonlaw.htm
Utah	http://www.commerce.utah.gov/dcp/education/lemonlaw.html
Vermont	http://www.aot.state.vt.us/dmv/LAWS/LEMONLAW/LAWSLemon.htm
Virginia	http://www.vdacs.virginia.gov/consumers/oca.html
Washington	http://www.atg.wa.gov/consumer/lemon/
West Virginia	http://www.wvs.state.wv.us/wvag/
Wisconsin	http://www.dot.wisconsin.gov/safety/consumer/rights/lemonlaw.htm
Wyoming	http://attorneygeneral.state.wy.us/consumer.htm

APPENDIX 15:
SAMPLE PRIVACY POLICY OUTLINE

1. IDENTITY OF THE WEB SITE ADMINISTRATORS

This is the Web site of [Company Name].

Our postal address is [Address].

We can be reached via email at [email address].

We can be reached by telephone at [telephone number].

2. FOR EACH VISITOR TO OUR WEB PAGE, OUR WEB SERVER AUTOMATICALLY RECOGNIZES: (CHOOSE ONE)

The consumer's domain name and email address (where possible);

Only the consumer's domain name, but not the email address (where possible);

No information regarding the domain or email address; or

Other [please explain].

3. WE COLLECT: (CHOOSE ALL THAT APPLY)

Only the domain name, but not the email address of visitors to our Web page;

The domain name and email address (where possible) of visitors to our Web page;

The email addresses of those who post messages to our bulletin board;

The email addresses of those who communicate with us via email;

The email addresses of those who make postings to our chat areas;

Aggregate information on what pages consumers access or visit;

User-specific information on what pages consumers access or visit;

Information volunteered by the consumer, such as survey information and/or site registrations;

No information on consumers who browse our Web page; and/or

Other [please explain].

4. THE INFORMATION WE COLLECT IS: (CHOOSE ALL THAT APPLY)

Used for internal review and is then discarded;

Used to improve the content of our Web page;

Used to customize the content and/or layout of our page for each individual visitor;

Used to notify visitors about updates to our Web site;

Used by us to contact consumers for marketing purposes;

Shared with other reputable organizations to help them contact consumers for marketing purposes;

Not shared with other organizations for commercial purposes; and/or

Other [please explain].

5. WITH RESPECT TO COOKIES:

We do not set any cookies; or

We use cookies to: (choose all that apply)

Store visitors preferences;

Record session information, such as items that consumers add to their shopping cart;

Record user-specific information on what pages users access or visit;

Alert visitors to new areas that we think might be of interest to them when they return to our site;

To record past activity at a site in order to provide better service when visitors return to our site;

Ensure that visitors are not repeatedly sent the same banner ads;

Customize Web page content on visitors' browser type or other information that the visitor sends; and/or

Other [please explain].

6. IF YOU DO NOT WANT TO RECEIVE EMAIL FROM US IN THE FUTURE, PLEASE TELL US THAT YOU DO NOT WANT TO RECEIVE EMAIL FROM OUR COMPANY AND PLEASE LET US KNOW BY: (CHOOSE ALL THAT APPLY)

Sending us email at the above address;

Calling us at the above telephone number;

Writing to us at the above address;

Visiting the following URL; and/or

Other [please explain].

7. FROM TIME TO TIME, WE MAKE THE EMAIL ADDRESSES OF THOSE WHO ACCESS OUR SITE AVAILABLE TO OTHER REPUTABLE ORGANIZATIONS WHOSE PRODUCTS OR SERVICES WE THINK YOU MIGHT FIND INTERESTING. IF YOU DO NOT WANT US TO SHARE YOUR EMAIL ADDRESS WITH OTHER COMPANIES OR ORGANIZATIONS, PLEASE TELL US THAT YOU DO NOT WANT US TO SHARE YOUR EMAIL ADDRESS WITH OTHER COMPANIES, AND LET US KNOW BY: (CHOOSE ALL THAT APPLY)

Sending us email at the above address;

Calling us at the above telephone number;

writing to us at the above address;

Visiting the following URL; and/or

Other (please explain).

8. FROM TIME TO TIME, WE MAKE OUR CUSTOMER EMAIL LIST AVAILABLE TO OTHER REPUTABLE ORGANIZATIONS WHOSE PRODUCTS OR SERVICES WE THINK YOU MIGHT FIND INTERESTING. IF YOU DO NOT WANT US TO SHARE YOUR EMAIL ADDRESS WITH OTHER COMPANIES OR ORGANIZATIONS, PLEASE LET US KNOW BY: (CHOOSE ALL THAT APPLY)

Sending us email at the above address;

Calling us at the above telephone number;

Writing to us at the above address;

Visiting the following URL; and/or

Other (please explain).

9. IF YOU SUPPLY US WITH YOUR POSTAL ADDRESS ONLINE-: (CHOOSE EITHER OPTION 1 OR A COMBINATION OF OPTIONS 2 AND 3)

(1) you will only receive the information for which you provided us your address;

(2) you may receive periodic mailings from us with information on new products and services or upcoming events.

If you do not wish to receive such mailings, please let us know by:

(choose all that apply)

Sending us email at the above address;

Calling us at the above telephone number;

Writing to us at the above address;

Visiting the following URL; and/or

Other (please explain).

(3) you may receive mailings from other reputable companies. You can, however, have your name put on our do-not-share list by:

(choose all that apply)

Sending us email at the above address;

Calling us at the above telephone number;

Writing to us at the above address;

Visiting the following URL; and/or

Other (please explain).

Please provide us with your exact name and address. We will be sure your name is removed from the list we share with other organizations.

10. PERSONS WHO SUPPLY US WITH THEIR TELEPHONE NUMBERS ONLINE: (CHOOSE ALL THAT APPLY)

Will only receive telephone contact from us with information regarding orders they have placed online-; and/or

May receive telephone contact from us with information regarding new products and services or upcoming events. If you do not wish to receive such telephone calls, please let us know by: (choose all that apply)

Sending us email at the above address;

Calling us at the above telephone number;

Writing to us at the above address;

Visiting the following URL; and/or

Other (please explain)

May receive telephone contact from other reputable companies. You can, however, have your name put on our do-not-share list by: (choose all that apply)

Sending us email at the above address;

Calling us at the above telephone number;

Writing to us at the above address;

Visiting the following URL; and/or

Other (please explain)

Please provide us with your name and phone number. We will be sure your name is removed from the list we share with other organizations.

11. AD SERVERS: (CHOOSE ONE)

We do not partner with or have special relationships with any ad server companies; or

To try and bring you offers that are of interest to you, we have relationships with other companies that we allow to place ads on our Web pages. As a result of your visit to our site, ad server companies may collect information such as your domain type, your IP address, and clickstream information. For further information, consult the privacy policies of:

[List the URLs for the privacy statements of the ad server companies with whom you have contracted or partnered].

12. FROM TIME TO TIME, WE MAY USE CUSTOMER INFORMATION FOR NEW, UNANTICIPATED USES NOT PREVIOUSLY DISCLOSED IN OUR PRIVACY NOTICE. IF OUR INFORMATION PRACTICES CHANGE AT SOME TIME IN THE FUTURE: (CHOOSE ALL THAT APPLY)

We will contact you before we use your data for these new purposes to notify you of the policy change and to provide you with the ability to opt out of these new uses;

We will post the policy changes to our Web site to notify you of these changes and provide you with the ability to opt out of these new uses. If you are concerned about how your information is used, you should check back at our Web site periodically;

We will use for these new purposes only data collected from the time of the policy change forward;

Customers may prevent their information from being used for purposes other than those for which it was originally collected by:

Sending us email at the above address;

Calling us at the above telephone number;

Writing to us at the above address;

Visiting the following URL; or

Other (please explain).

13. UPON REQUEST WE PROVIDE SITE VISITORS WITH ACCESS TO: (CHOOSE ALL THAT APPLY)

All information [including proprietary information] that we maintain about them;

Financial information (e.g., credit card account information) that we maintain about them;

Unique identifier information (e.g., customer number or password) that we maintain about them;

Transaction information (e.g., dates on which customers made purchases, amounts and types of purchases) that we maintain about them;

Communications that the consumer/visitor has directed to our site (e.g., emails, customer inquiries);

Contact information (e.g., name, address, phone number) that we maintain about them;

A description of information that we maintain about them;

No information that we have collected and that we maintain about them;

Consumers can access this information by (choose all that apply)

Sending us email at the above address;

Calling us at the above telephone number;

Writing to us at the above address;

Visiting the following URL; and/or

Other (please explain).

14. UPON REQUEST WE OFFER VISITORS:

No ability to have factual inaccuracies corrected in information that we maintain about them; or

The ability to have inaccuracies corrected in: (choose all that apply)

Contact information;

Financial information;

Unique identifiers;

Transaction information;

Communications that the consumer/visitor has directed to the site; and/or

All information that we maintain.

Consumers can have this information corrected by: (choose all that apply)

Sending us email at the above address;

Calling us at the above telephone number;

Writing to us at the above address;

Visiting the following URL; and/or

Other (please explain).

15. SECURITY: (CHOOSE ALL THAT APPLY)

We always use industry-standard encryption technologies when transferring and receiving consumer data exchanged with our site:

When we transfer and receive certain types of sensitive information such as financial or health information, we redirect visitors to a secure server and will notify visitors through a pop-up screen on our site;

We have appropriate security measures in place in our physical facilities to protect against the loss, misuse, or alteration of information that we have collected from you at our site; and/or

Other (please explain).

16. ENFORCEMENT:

If you feel that this site is not following its stated information policy, you may contact:

[Company Name] at the above addresses or phone number;

The DMA's Committee on Ethical Business Practices at mgoldberger@the-DMA.org;

State or local chapters of the Better Business Bureau;

State or local consumer protection office;

The Federal Trade Commission by telephone at: 202-FTC-HELP (202-382-4357); or electronically at http://www.ftc.gov/to/romap2.htm; and/or

Other [please explain].

Source: The Direct Marketing Association.

APPENDIX 16:
FTC ID THEFT AFFIDAVIT

Instructions for
Completing the ID Theft Affidavit

To make certain that you do not become responsible for any debts incurred by an identity thief, you must prove to each of the companies where accounts were opened or used in your name that you didn't create the debt.

A group of credit grantors, consumer advocates, and attorneys at the Federal Trade Commission (FTC) developed an ID Theft Affidavit to make it easier for fraud victims to report information. While many companies accept this affidavit, others require that you submit more or different forms. Before you send the affidavit, contact each company to find out if they accept it.

It will be necessary to provide the information in this affidavit anywhere a **new** account was opened in your name. The information will enable the companies to investigate the fraud and decide the outcome of your claim. If someone made unauthorized charges to an **existing** account, call the company for instructions.

This affidavit has two parts:
- **Part One** — the ID Theft Affidavit — is where you report general information about yourself and the theft.
- **Part Two** — the Fraudulent Account Statement — is where you describe the fraudulent account(s) opened in your name. Use a separate Fraudulent Account Statement for each company you need to write to.

When you send the affidavit to the companies, attach copies (NOT originals) of any supporting documents (for example, driver's license or police report). Before submitting your affidavit, review the disputed account(s) with family members or friends who may have information about the account(s) or access to them.

Complete this affidavit as soon as possible. Many creditors ask that you send it within two weeks. Delays on your part could slow the investigation.

Be as accurate and complete as possible. You may choose not to provide some of the information requested. However, incorrect or incomplete information will slow the process of investigating your claim and absolving the debt. Print clearly.

When you have finished completing the affidavit, mail a copy to each creditor, bank, or company that provided the thief with the unauthorized credit, goods, or services you describe. Attach a copy of the Fraudulent Account Statement with information only on accounts opened at the institution to which you are sending the packet, as well as any other supporting documentation you are able to provide.

Send the appropriate documents to each company by certified mail, return receipt requested, so you can prove that it was received. The companies will review your claim and send you a written response telling you the outcome of their investigation. Keep a copy of everything you submit.

If you are unable to complete the affidavit, a legal guardian or someone with power of attorney may complete it for you. Except as noted, the information you provide will be used only by the company to process your affidavit, investigate the events you report, and help stop further fraud. If this affidavit is requested in a lawsuit, the company might have to provide it to the requesting party. Completing this affidavit does not guarantee that the identity thief will be prosecuted or that the debt will be cleared.

DO NOT SEND AFFIDAVIT TO THE FTC OR ANY OTHER
GOVERNMENT AGENCY

If you haven't already done so, report the fraud to the following organizations:

1. Any one of the nationwide consumer reporting companies to place a fraud alert on your credit report. Fraud alerts can help prevent an identity thief from opening any more accounts in your name. The company you call is required to contact the other two, which will place an alert on their versions of your report, too.

  - **Equifax:** 1-800-525-6285; www.equifax.com

  - **Experian:** 1-888-EXPERIAN (397-3742); www.experian.com

  - **TransUnion:** 1-800-680-7289; www.transunion.com

In addition to placing the fraud alert, the three consumer reporting companies will send you free copies of your credit reports, and, if you ask, they will display only the last four digits of your Social Security number on your credit reports.

2. The security or fraud department of each company where you know, or believe, accounts have been tampered with or opened fraudulently. Close the accounts. Follow up in writing, and include copies (NOT originals) of supporting documents. *It's important to notify credit card companies and banks in writing.* Send your letters by certified mail, return receipt requested, so you can document what the company received and when. Keep a file of your correspondence and enclosures.

When you open new accounts, use new Personal Identification Numbers (PINs) and passwords. Avoid using easily available information like your mother's maiden name, your birth date, the last four digits of your Social Security number or your phone number, or a series of consecutive numbers.

3. Your local police or the police in the community where the identity theft took place to file a report. Get a copy of the police report or, at the very least, the number of the report. It can help you deal with creditors who need proof of the crime. If the police are reluctant to take your report, ask to file a "Miscellaneous Incidents" report, or try another jurisdiction, like your state police. You also can check with your state Attorney General's office to find out if state law requires the police to take reports for identity theft. Check the Blue Pages of your telephone directory for the phone number or check www.naag.org for a list of state Attorneys General.

4. The Federal Trade Commission. By sharing your identity theft complaint with the FTC, you will provide important information that can help law enforcement officials across the nation track down identity thieves and stop them. The FTC also can refer victims' complaints to other government agencies and companies for further action, as well as investigate companies for violations of laws that the FTC enforces.

You can file a complaint online at **www.consumer.gov/idtheft**. If you don't have Internet access, call the FTC's Identity Theft Hotline, toll-free: 1-877-IDTHEFT (438-4338); TTY: 1-866-653-4261; or write: Identity Theft Clearinghouse, Federal Trade Commission, 600 Pennsylvania Avenue, NW, Washington, DC 20580.

DO NOT SEND AFFIDAVIT TO THE FTC OR ANY OTHER GOVERNMENT AGENCY

ID Theft Affidavit

Victim Information

(1) My full legal name is _____
                            (First)   (Middle)   (Last)   (Jr., Sr., III)

(2) (If different from above) When the events described in this affidavit took place, I was known as

_____
(First)   (Middle)   (Last)   (Jr., Sr., III)

(3) My date of birth is _____
                   (day/month/year)

(4) My Social Security number is_____

(5) My driver's license or identification card state and number are_____

(6) My current address is _____

City _____ State _____ Zip Code _____

(7) I have lived at this address since _____
                             (month/year)

(8) (If different from above) When the events described in this affidavit took place, my address was

_____

City _____ State _____ Zip Code _____

(9) I lived at the address in Item 8 from _____ until _____
                                  (month/year)   (month/year)

(10) My daytime telephone number is (____)_____

My evening telephone number is (____)_____

DO NOT SEND AFFIDAVIT TO THE FTC OR ANY OTHER GOVERNMENT AGENCY

Name _____ Phone number _____ *Page 2*

Check all that apply for items 11 - 17:

(11) ❑ I did not authorize anyone to use my name or personal information to seek the money, credit, loans, goods or services described in this report.

(12) ❑ I did not receive any benefit, money, goods or services as a result of the events described in this report.

(13) ❑ My identification documents (for example, credit cards; birth certificate; driver's license; Social Security card; etc.) were ❑ stolen ❑ lost on or about _____.
(day/month/year)

(14) ❑ To the best of my knowledge and belief, the following person(s) used my information (for example, my name, address, date of birth, existing account numbers, Social Security number, mother's maiden name, etc.) or identification documents to get money, credit, loans, goods or services without my knowledge or authorization:

_____   _____
Name (if known)   Name (if known)

_____   _____
Address (if known)   Address (if known)

_____   _____
Phone number(s) (if known)   Phone number(s) (if known)

_____   _____
Additional information (if known)   Additional information (if known)

(15) ❑ I do NOT know who used my information or identification documents to get money, credit, loans, goods or services without my knowledge or authorization.

(16) ❑ Additional comments: (For example, description of the fraud, which documents or information were used or how the identity thief gained access to your information.)

_____

_____

_____

_____

(Attach additional pages as necessary.)

DO NOT SEND AFFIDAVIT TO THE FTC OR ANY OTHER GOVERNMENT AGENCY

Victim's Law Enforcement Actions

(17) (check one) I ❏ am   ❏ am not   willing to assist in the prosecution of the person(s) who committed this fraud.

(18) (check one) I ❏ am   ❏ am not   authorizing the release of this information to law enforcement for the purpose of assisting them in the investigation and prosecution of the person(s) who committed this fraud.

(19) (check all that apply) I ❏ have   ❏ have not   reported the events described in this affidavit to the police or other law enforcement agency. The police ❏ did ❏ did not   write a report. *In the event you have contacted the police or other law enforcement agency, please complete the following:*

(Agency #1)	(Officer/Agency personnel taking report)
(Date of report)	(Report number, if any)
(Phone number)	(email address, if any)
(Agency #2)	(Officer/Agency personnel taking report)
(Date of report)	(Report number, if any)
(Phone number)	(email address, if any)

Documentation Checklist

Please indicate the supporting documentation you are able to provide to the companies you plan to notify. Attach copies (NOT originals) to the affidavit before sending it to the companies.

(20) ❏ A copy of a valid government-issued photo-identification card (for example, your driver's license, state-issued ID card or your passport). If you are under 16 and don't have a photo-ID, you may submit a copy of your birth certificate or a copy of your official school records showing your enrollment and place of residence.

(21) ❏ Proof of residency during the time the disputed bill occurred, the loan was made or the other event took place (for example, a rental/lease agreement in your name, a copy of a utility bill or a copy of an insurance bill).

DO NOT SEND AFFIDAVIT TO THE FTC OR ANY OTHER GOVERNMENT AGENCY

(22) ❑ A copy of the report you filed with the police or sheriff's department. If you are unable to obtain a report or report number from the police, please indicate that in Item 19. Some companies only need the report number, not a copy of the report. You may want to check with each company.

Signature

I certify that, to the best of my knowledge and belief, all the information on and attached to this affidavit is true, correct, and complete and made in good faith. I also understand that is affidavit or the information it contains may be made available to federal, state, and/or local law enforcement agencies for such action within their jurisdiction as they deem appropriate. I understand that knowingly making any false or fraudulent statement or representation to the government may constitute a violation of 18 U.S.C. §1001 or other federal, state, or local criminal statutes, and may result in imposition of a fine or imprisonment or both.

_____   _____
(signature)   (date signed)

_____
(Notary)

[Check with each company. Creditors sometimes require notarization. If they do not, please have one witness (non-relative) sign below that you completed and signed this affidavit.]

Witness:

_____   _____
(signature)   (printed name)

_____   _____
(date)   (telephone number)

DO NOT SEND AFFIDAVIT TO THE FTC OR ANY OTHER GOVERNMENT AGENCY

Name _____ Phone number _____ Page 5

Fraudulent Account Statement

> **Completing this Statement**
> - Make as many copies of this page as you need. **Complete a separate page for each company you're notifying and only send it to that company.** Include a copy of your signed affidavit.
> - List only the account(s) you're disputing with the company receiving this form. **See the example below.**
> - If a collection agency sent you a statement, letter or notice about the fraudulent account, attach a copy of that document (**NOT** the original).

I declare (check all that apply):

❏ As a result of the event(s) described in the ID Theft Affidavit, the following account(s) was/were opened at your company in my name without my knowledge, permission or authorization using my personal information or identifying documents:

Creditor Name/Address (the company that opened the account or provided the goods or services)	Account Number	Type of unauthorized credit/goods/services provided by creditor (if known)	Date issued or opened (if known)	Amount/Value provided (the amount charged or the cost of the goods/services)
Example Example National Bank 22 Main Street Columbus, Ohio 22722	01234567-89	auto loan	01/05/2002	$25,500.00

❏ During the time of the accounts described above, I had the following account open with your company:

Billing name _____

Billing address _____

Account number _____

DO NOT SEND AFFIDAVIT TO THE FTC OR ANY OTHER GOVERNMENT AGENCY

APPENDIX 17:
STATE TENANTS RIGHTS LAWS

STATE	STATUTE
Alabama	Ala. Code §§ 35-9-1 to -100
Alaska	Alaska Stat. §§ 34.03.010 to.380
Arizona	Ariz. Rev. Stat. Ann. §§ 12-1171 to -1183; §§ 33-1301 to -1381
Arkansas	Ark. Code Ann. §§ 18-16-101 to -306
California	Cal. [Civ.] Code §§ 1925-1954, 1961-1962.7, 1995.010-1997.270
Colorado	Colo. Rev. Stat. §§ 38-12-101 to -104, -301 to -302
Connecticut	Conn. Gen. Stat. Ann. §§ 47a-1 to -51
Delaware	Del. Code. Ann. tit. 25* §§ 5101-7013
District of Columbia	D.C. Code Ann. §§ 42-3201 to -4097, -3501.01 to -3509.03
Florida	Fla. Stat. Ann. §§ 83.40-.66
Georgia	Ga. Code Ann. §§ 44-7-1 to -81
Hawaii	Haw. Rev. Stat. §§ 521-1 to -78
Idaho	Idaho Code §§ 6-301 to -324 and §§ 55-201 to -313
Illinois	Ill. Comp. Stat. ch. 765 para. 705/0.01-740/5
Indiana	Ind. Code Ann. §§ 32-7-1-1 to 37-7-9-10
Iowa	Iowa Code Ann. §§ 562A.1-.36
Kansas	Kan. Stat. Ann. §§ 58-2501 to -2573
Kentucky	Ky. Rev. Stat. Ann. §§ 383.010-.715

STATE	STATUTE
Louisiana	La. Rev. Stat. Ann. §§ 9:3201-:3259, La. Civ. Code Ann. art. 2669-2742
Maine	Me. Rev. Stat. Ann. tit. 14* §§ 6001-6046
Maryland	Md. Real Prop. Code Ann.
Massachusetts	Mass. Gen. Laws Ann. ch. 186 §§ 1-21
Michigan	Mich. Comp. Laws Ann. §§ 554.601-.640
Minnesota	Minn. Stat. Ann. §§ 504B.001 to 504B.471
Mississippi	Miss. Code Ann. §§ 89-8-1 to -27
Missouri	Mo. Ann. Stat. §§ 441.005 to.880, and §§ 535.150-.300
Montana	Mont. Code Ann. §§ 70-24-101 to -25-206
Nebraska	Neb. Rev. Stat. §§ 76-1401 to -1449
Nevada	Nev. Rev. Stat. Ann. §§ 118A.010-.520
New Hampshire.	N.H. Rev. Stat. Ann. §§ 540:1 to 540:29; 540-A:1-540-A:8
New Jersey	N.J. Stat. Ann. §§ 46:8-1 to-49
New Mexico	N.M. Stat. Ann. §§ 47-8-1 to -51
New York	N.Y. Real Property Law ("RPL") §§ 220-238; Real Property Actions and Proceedings Law ("RPAPL")§§ 701-853; Multiple Dwelling Law ("MDL") all; Multiple Residence Law ("MRL") all; General Obligation Law ("GOL") §§ 7-103-108
North Carolina	N.C. Gen. Stat. §§ 42-1 to 42-14.2; 42-25-6 to 42-76
North Dakota	N.D. Cent. Code §§ 47-16-01 to -41
Ohio	Ohio Rev. Code Ann. §§ 5321.01-.19
Oklahoma	Okla. Stat. Ann. tit. 41
Oregon	Or. Rev. Stat. §§ 90.100-.450
Pennsylvania	Pa. Stat. Ann. tit. 68, §§ 250.101-.510-B
Rhode Island	R.I. Gen. Laws §§ 34-18-1 to -57
South Carolina	S.C. Code Ann. §§ 27-40-10 to -910
South Dakota	S.D. Codified Laws Ann. §§ 43-32-1 to -29
Tennessee	Tenn. Code Ann. §§ 66-28-101 to -520
Texas	Tex. Prop. Code Ann. §§ 91.001-92.354
Utah	Utah Code Ann. §§ 57-17-1 to -5, -22-1 to -6

STATE	STATUTE
Vermont	Vt. Stat Ann. tit. 9, §§ 4451-4468
Virginia	Va. Code Ann. §§ 55-218.1 to -248.40
Washington	Wash. Rev. Code Ann. §§ 59.04.010-.900,.18.010-.911
West Virginia	W. Va. Code §§ 37-6-1 to -30
Wisconsin	Wis. Stat. Ann. §§ 704.01-.45
Wyoming	Wyo. Stat. §§ 1-21-1201 to -1211; 34-2-128 to -129

APPENDIX 18:
HUD FAIR HOUSING DISCRIMINATION
COMPLAINT FORM

OMB Approval No. 2529-0011 (expires 11/30/2007)

U.S. Department of Housing and Urban Development
Office of Fair Housing and Equal Opportunity

Are you a Victim of Housing Discrimination?

Fair Housing is Your Right!

If you have been denied your housing rights ... you may have experienced housing discrimination.

Previous Versions Obsolete   Page 1 of 7   form **HUD-903.1** (7/2004)

How do you recognize Housing Discrimination?

Under the Fair Housing Act, It is Against the Law to:

- Refuse to rent to you or sell you housing
- Tell you housing is unavailable when in fact it is available
- Show you apartments or homes in certain neighborhoods only
- Advertise housing to preferred groups of people only
- Refuse to provide you with information regarding mortgage loans, deny you a mortgage loan, or impose different terms or conditions on a mortgage loan
- Deny you property insurance
- Conduct property appraisals in a discriminatory manner
- Refuse to make certain modifications or accommodations for persons with a mental or physical disability, including persons recovering from alcohol and substance abuse, and HIV/AIDS-related illnesses
- Fail to design and construct housing in an accessible manner
- Harass, coerce, intimidate, or interfere with anyone exercising or assisting someone else with their fair housing rights

Based on these factors...

- Race
- Color
- National origin
- Religion
- Sex
- Familial status (families with children under the age of 18, or who are expecting a child), or
- Handicap (if you or someone close to you has a disability)

If you don't report discrimination,
it can't be stopped!

Housing Discrimination Information Form

- If you believe your rights have been violated, HUD or a State or local fair housing agency is ready to help you file a complaint.

- You have one year from the date of the alleged act of discrimination to file your complaint.

- After your information is received, we will contact you to discuss the concerns you raise.

Instructions: (Please type or print.) Read this form carefully. Try to answer all questions. If you do not know the answer or a question does not apply to you, leave the space blank. You have one year from the date of the alleged discrimination to file a complaint. Your form should be signed and dated. Use reverse side of this page if you need more space to respond.

Keep this information for your records.

Date you mailed your information to HUD:(mm/dd/yyyy)

Address to which you sent the information:
   Street:

   City: State: Zip Code:

If you have not heard from HUD or a fair housing agency within three weeks from the date you mail this form, you may call to inquire about the status of your complaint. See addresses and telephone listings on the last page.

Your Name:	Best time to call:	Your Daytime Phone No:
Your Address:		Evening Phone No:
City:	State:	Zip Code:

Who else can we call if we cannot reach you?

1 Contact's Name:	Daytime Phone No:
Best time to call:	Evening Phone No:
2 Contact's Name:	Daytime Phone No:
Best time to call:	Evening Phone No:

1. **What** happened to you? How were you discriminated against? For example: were you refused an opportunity to rent or buy housing? Denied a loan? Told that housing was not available when in fact it was? Treated differently from others seeking housing? State briefly what happened.

2. **Why** do you believe you are being discriminated against?

   It is a violation of the law to deny you your housing rights for any of the following factors: • race • color • religion • sex • national origin • familial status (families with children under 18) • disability.

   For example: were you denied housing **because of** your race? Were you denied a mortgage loan **because of** your religion? Or turned down for an apartment **because** you have children? Were you harassed because you assisted someone in obtaining their fair housing rights? Briefly explain why you think your housing rights were denied **because of** any the factors listed above.

3. **Who** do you believe discriminated against you? Was it a landlord, owner, bank, real estate agent, broker, company, or organization?

Name:

Address:

4. **Where** did the alleged act of discrimination occur? Provide the address. For example: Was it at a rental unit? Single family home? Public or Assisted Housing? A Mobile Home? Did it occur at a bank or other lending institution?

Address:

City: State: Zip Code:

5. **When** did the last act of discrimination occur?
   Enter the date (mm/dd/yyyy) _____
   Is the alleged discrimination continuous or on going?   ☐ Yes   ☐ No

Signature: Date:(mm/dd/yyyy)

X _____

Send this form to HUD or to the fair housing agency where the alleged act of discrimination occurred.
If you are unable to complete this form, you may call the office nearest you.
See addresses and telephone numbers listed on the back page.

The information collected here will be used to investigate and to process housing discrimination complaints. The information may be disclosed to the United States Department of Justice for its use in the filing of pattern and practice suits of housing discrimination or the prosecution of the person(s) who committed the discrimination where violence is involved; and to State or local fair housing agencies that administer substantially equivalent fair housing laws for complaint processing.

Public Reporting Burden for this collection of information is estimated to average 20 minutes per response, including the time for reviewing instructions, searching existing data sources, gathering and maintaining the data needed, and completing and reviewing the collection of information.

Disclosure of this information is voluntary. Failure to provide some or all of the requested information will result in delay or denial of HUD assistance.

This agency may not collect this information, and you are not required to complete this form, unless it displays a currently valid OMB control number.

Privacy Act Statement The Department of Housing and Urban Development is authorized to collect this information by Title VIII of the Civil Rights Act of 1968, as amended by the Fair Housing Amendments Act of 1988, (P.L. 100-430); Title VI of the Civil Rights Act of 1964, (P.L. 88-352); Section 504 of the Rehabilitation Act of 1973, as amended, (P.L. 93-112); Section 109 of Title I - Housing and Community Development Act of 1974, as amended, (P.L. 97-35); Americans with Disabilities Act of 1990, (P.L. 101-336); and by the Age Discrimination Act of 1975, as amended, (42 U.S.C. 6103).

For Connecticut, Maine, Massachusetts, New Hampshire, Rhode Island, and Vermont:

NEW ENGLAND OFFICE
(Marcella_Brown@hud.gov)
Fair Housing Enforcement Center
U.S. Department of Housing and Urban Development
Thomas P. O'Neill, Jr. Federal Building
10 Causeway Street, Room 321
Boston, MA 02222-1092
Telephone (617) 994-8300 or
1-800-827-5005
Fax (617) 565-7313 • TTY (617) 565-5453

For New Jersey and New York

New York/New Jersey Office
(Stanley_Seidenfeld@hud.gov)
Fair Housing Enforcement Center
U.S. Department of Housing and Urban Development
26 Federal Plaza, Room 3532
New York, NY 10278-0068
Telephone (212) 264-1290 or
1-800-496-4294
Fax (212) 264-9829 • TTY (212) 264-0927

For Delaware, District of Columbia, Maryland, Pennsylvania, Virginia, and West Virginia

MID-ATLANTIC OFFICE
(Wanda_Nieves@hud.gov)
Fair Housing Enforcement Center
U.S. Department of Housing and Urban Development
The Wanamaker Building
100 Penn Square East
Philadelphia, PA 19107-9344
Telephone (215) 656-0662 or
1-888-799-2085
Fax (215) 656-3419 • TTY (215) 656-3450

For Alabama, the Caribbean, Florida, Georgia, Kentucky, Mississippi, North Carolina, South Carolina, and Tennessee:

SOUTHEAST/CARIBBEAN OFFICE
(Gregory_L._King@hud.gov)
Fair Housing Enforcement Center
U.S. Department of Housing and Urban Development
Five Points Plaza
40 Marietta Street, 16th Floor
Atlanta, GA 30303-2806
Telephone (404) 331-5140 or
1-800-440-8091
Fax (404) 331-1021 • TTY (404) 730-2654

For Illinois, Indiana, Michigan, Minnesota, Ohio, and Wisconsin:

MIDWEST OFFICE
(Barbara_Knox@hud.gov)
Fair Housing Enforcement Center
U.S. Department of Housing and Urban Development
Ralph H. Metcalfe Federal Building
77 West Jackson Boulevard, Room 2101
Chicago, IL 60604-3507
Telephone (312) 353-7776 or
1-800-765-9372
Fax (312) 886-2837 • TTY (312) 353-7143

For Arkansas, Louisiana, New Mexico, Oklahoma, and Texas:

SOUTHWEST OFFICE
(Thurman_G._Miles@hud.gov or Garry_L._Sweeney@hud.gov)
Fair Housing Enforcement Center
U.S. Department of Housing and Urban Development
801 North Cherry, 27th Floor
Fort Worth, TX 76102
Telephone (817) 978-5900 or
1-888-560-8913
Fax (817) 978-5876 or 5851 • TTY (817) 978-5595

Previous Versions Obsolete   Page 6 of 7   form **HUD-903.1** (7/2004)

For Alaska, Idaho, Oregon, and Washington:

For Iowa, Kansas, Missouri and Nebraska:

GREAT PLAINS OFFICE
(Robbie_Herndon@hud.gov)

Fair Housing Enforcement Center
U.S. Department of Housing and
Urban Development
Gateway Tower II
400 State Avenue, Room 200, 4th
Floor
Kansas City, KS 66101-2406
Telephone (913) 551-6958 or
1-800-743-5323
Fax (913) 551-6856 • TTY (913)
551-6972

*For Colorado, Montana, North
Dakota, South Dakota, Utah, and
Wyoming:*

ROCKY MOUNTAINS OFFICE
(Sharon_L._Santoya@hud.gov)

Fair Housing Enforcement Center
U.S. Department of Housing and
Urban Development
633 17th Street
Denver, CO 80202-3690
Telephone (303) 672-5437 or
1-800-877-7353
Fax (303) 672-5026 • TTY (303)
672-5248

*For Arizona, California, Hawaii,
and Nevada:*

PACIFIC/HAWAII OFFICE
(Charles_Hauptman@hud.gov)

Fair Housing Enforcement Center
U.S. Department of Housing and
Urban Development
600 Harrison Street, 3rd Floor
San Francisco, CA 94107-1300
Telephone (415) 489-6524 or
1-800-347-3739
Fax (415) 489-6559 • TTY (415)
489-6564

NORTHWEST/ALASKA OFFICE
(Judith_Keeler@hud.gov)

Fair Housing Enforcement Center
U.S. Department of Housing and
Urban Development
Seattle Federal Office Building
909 First Avenue, Room 205
Seattle, WA 98104-1000
Telephone (206) 220-5170 or
1-800-877-0246
Fax (206) 220-5447 • TTY (206)
220-5185

**If after contacting the local office
nearest you, you still have
questions – you may contact HUD
further at***:*

U.S. Department of Housing and
Urban Development
Office of Fair Housing and Equal
Opportunity
451 7th Street, S.W., Room 5204
Washington, DC 20410-2000
Telephone (202) 708-0836 or
1-800-669-9777
Fax (202) 708-1425 • TTY 1-800-
927-9275

Consumer Rights Law   **205**

APPENDIX 19:
RULES FOR RETURNING SECURITY
DEPOSITS, BY STATE

STATE	DEADLINE
Alabama	No statutory deadline
Alaska	14 days if the tenant gives proper notice to terminate tenancy; 30 days if the tenant does not give proper notice
Arizona	14 days
Arkansas	30 days
California	Three weeks
Colorado	One month, unless lease agreement specifies longer period of time, which may be no more than 60 days; 72 hours, not counting weekends or holidays, if a hazardous condition involving gas equipment requires tenant to vacate
Connecticut	30 days, or within 15 days of receiving tenant's forwarding address, whichever is later
Delaware	20 days
District of Columbia	45 days
Florida	15 to 60 days depending on whether tenant disputes deductions
Georgia	One month
Hawaii	14 days
Idaho	21 days or up to 30 days if landlord and tenant agree
Illinois	30-45 days depending on whether tenant disputes deductions
Indiana	45 days

STATE	DEADLINE
Iowa	30 days
Kansas	30 days
Kentucky	30-60 days depending on whether tenant disputes deductions
Louisiana	One month
Maine	30 days if written rental agreement; 21 days if tenancy at will
Maryland	30-45 days depending on whether tenant has been evicted or has abandoned the premises
Massachusetts	30 days
Michigan	30 days
Minnesota	Three weeks after tenant leaves and landlord receives mailing address; five days if tenant must leave due to building condemnation
Mississippi	45 days
Missouri	30 days
Montana	30 days; 10 days if no deductions
Nebraska	14 days
Nevada	30 days
New Hampshire	30 days; for shared facilities, if the deposit is more than 30 days' rent, landlord must provide written agreement acknowledging receipt and specifying when deposit will be returned; if no written agreement, 20 days after tenant vacates
New Jersey	30 days; five days in case of fire, flood, condemnation, or evacuation
New Mexico	30 days
New York	Reasonable time
North Carolina	30 days
North Dakota	30 days
Ohio	30 days
Oklahoma	30 days
Oregon	31 days
Pennsylvania	30 days
Rhode Island	20 days

STATE	DEADLINE
South Carolina	30 days
South Dakota	Two weeks to return entire deposit or a portion and supply reasons for withholding; 45 days for a written, itemized accounting if tenant requests it
Tennessee	No statutory deadline
Texas	30 days
Utah	30 days, or within 15 days of receiving tenant's forwarding address, whichever is later Vermont, 14 days
Virginia	45 days
Washington	14 days
West Virginia	No statutory deadline
Wisconsin	21 days
Wyoming	30 days, or within 15 days of receiving tenant's forwarding address, whichever is later; 60 days if there is damage

GLOSSARY

Abuse of Process—The improper and malicious use of the criminal or civil process.

Acceptance—Acceptance refers to one's consent to the terms of an offer, which consent creates a contract.

Accord and Satisfaction—Accord and satisfaction refers to the payment of money, or other thing of value, which is usually less than the amount owed or demanded, in exchange for extinguishment of the debt.

Accrue—To occur or come into existence.

Action at Law—A judicial proceeding whereby one party prosecutes another for a wrong done.

Actionable—Giving rise to a cause of action.

Actual Damages—Actual damages are those damages directly referable to the breach or tortious act, and which can be readily proven to have been sustained, and for which the injured party should be compensated as a matter of right.

Additional Principal Payment—Additional money included with a loan payment to pay off the amount owed faster thus reducing the amount of interest paid.

Adhesion Contract—An adhesion contract is a standardized contract form offered to consumers of goods and services on a "take it or leave it" basis without affording the consumer a realistic opportunity to bargain, and under such conditions that infer coercion.

Affirmative Defense—In a pleading, a matter constituting a defense.

Agency—The relationship between a principal and agent, who is employed by the principal to perform certain acts dealing with third parties.

Agent—One who represents another known as the principal.

American Arbitration Association (AAA)—National organization of arbitrators from whose panel arbitrators are selected for labor and civil disputes.

Amortization—The process of satisfying a debt by making a series of equal payments of interest and principal over a period of time.

Annual Fee—A fee charged by a bank annually for use of a credit card.

Annual Percentage Rate (APR)—The annual percentage rate is the actual cost of borrowing money, expressed in the form of an annual rate to make it easy for one to compare the cost of borrowing money among several lenders.

Answer—In a civil proceeding, the principal pleading on the part of the defendant in response to the plaintiff's complaint.

Anticipatory Breach of Contract—A breach committed before the arrival of the actual time of required performance.

Antitrust Laws—Statutes designed to promote free competition in the market place.

Apparent Agency—Apparent agency refers to the situation when one person, whether or not authorized, reasonably appears to a third person, due to the manifestation of another, to be authorized to act as agent for such other.

Appearance—To come into court, personally or through an attorney, after being summoned.

Arbitration—The reference of a dispute to an impartial person chosen by the parties to the dispute who agree in advance to abide by the arbitrator's award issued after a hearing at which both parties have an opportunity to be heard.

Arbitration Clause—A clause inserted in a contract providing for compulsory arbitration in case of a dispute as to the rights or liabilities under such contract.

Arbitrator—A private, disinterested person, chosen by the parties to a disputed question, for the purpose of hearing their contention, and awarding judgment to the prevailing party.

Arrears—Payments which are due but not yet paid.

Arm's Length—Refers to the bargaining position of two parties that are unrelated to one another and have no other motivation for dealing other than to transact business in good faith.

As Is—Refers to the sale of an item for which the seller gives no warranties to the buyer and the buyer purchases the item and assumes the risk of its condition.

Asset—The entirety of a person's property, either real or personal.

Assignee—An assignee is a person to whom an assignment is made, also known as a grantee.

Assignment—An assignment is the transfer of an interest in a right or property from one party to another.

Authorized User—Any person to whom the credit card holder gives permission to use a credit card account.

Average Daily Balance—The method by which most credit cards calculate the credit card holder's payment, computed by adding each day's balance and dividing the total by the number of days in a billing cycle.

Award—The final and binding decision of an arbitrator, made in writing and enforceable in court under state and federal statutes.

Bad Faith—A willful failure to comply with one's statutory or contractual obligations.

Bad Title—A title which is not legally sufficient to transfer property to the purchaser.

Bankrupt—The state or condition of one who is unable to pay his debts as they are, or become, due.

Bankruptcy—The legal process governed by federal law designed to assist the debtor in a new financial start while insuring fairness among creditors.

Bankruptcy Code—Refers to the Bankruptcy Act of 1978, the federal law which governs bankruptcy actions.

Bargain—A voluntary and mutual agreement between two parties for the exchange or purchase of some specified goods.

Bid—An offer to buy goods or services at a stated price.

Bilateral Contract—A bilateral contract is one containing mutual promises between the parties to the contract, each being termed both a promisor and a promisee.

Bill—As referred to in commercial law, an account for goods sold, services rendered and work done.

Billing Period—The number of days used to calculate interest on a loan or credit card.

Billing Statement—The monthly bill sent by a credit card issuer to the customer.

Bill of Sale—A written agreement by which the exchange of personal property is made.

Boilerplate—Refers to standard language found almost universally in certain documents.

Bona Fide Purchaser—One who pays valuable consideration for a purchase.

Breach of Contract—The failure, without any legal excuse, to perform any promise which forms the whole or the part of a contract.

Breach of Duty—In a general sense, any violation or omission of a legal or moral duty.

Breach of Warranty—An infraction of an express or implied agreement as to the title, quality, content or condition of a thing which is sold.

Burden of Proof—The duty of a party to substantiate an allegation or issue to convince the trier of fact as to the truth of their claim.

Capacity—Capacity is the legal qualification concerning the ability of one to understand the nature and effects of one's acts.

Cash Flow—The difference between cash inflow and cash outflow computed over a certain period of time.

Cash Inflow—Cash-based income, such as your salary.

Cash Outflow—Expenses, including mortgage payments, living expenses, credit card payments, etc.

Cause of Action—The factual basis for bringing a lawsuit.

Caveat Emptor—Latin for "let the buyer beware."

Charge-Off—A debt deemed uncollectible by the creditor and reported as a bad debt to a credit reporting agency.

Chattel—Any tangible, movable piece of personal property as opposed to real property.

Check—A draft drawn upon a bank and payable on demand, signed by the maker or drawer, and containing an unconditional promise to pay a certain sum of money to the payee.

Civil Action—An action maintained to protect a private civil right as opposed to a criminal action.

Civil Court—The court designed to resolve disputes arising under the common law and civil statutes.

Civil Law—Law which applies to non-criminal actions.

Clean Hands Doctrine—The concept that claimants who seek equitable relief must not themselves have indulged in any impropriety in relation to the transaction upon which relief is sought.

Closed-End credit—Credit that requires the borrower to repay the loaned amount without the ability to borrow any of the amount repaid.

Collateral—Property which is pledged as additional security for a debt, such as a loan.

Confession of Judgment—An admission of a debt by the debtor which may be entered as a judgment without the necessity of a formal legal proceeding.

Consequential Damages—Consequential damages are those damages which are caused by an injury, but which are not a necessary result of the injury, and must be specially pleaded and proven in order to be awarded.

Consideration—Something of value exchanged between parties to a contract, which is a requirement of a valid contract.

Consumer—A buyer of any consumer product.

Consumer Bankruptcy—A bankruptcy case filed to reduce or eliminate debts that are primarily consumer debts.

Consumer Credit Counseling Service—A service that offers counseling to consumers and serves as a intermediary with creditors regarding debt repayment and budget planning.

Consumer Credit—Loans for personal or household use as opposed to business or commercial lending.

Consumer Debts—Debts incurred for personal needs.

Consumer Product—Any tangible personal property which is distributed in commerce and which is normally used for personal, family, or household purposes.

Contract—A contract is an agreement between two or more persons which creates an obligation to do or not to do a particular thing.

Co-Signer—A person who signs a promissory note that is also signed by one or more other parties, and for which both parties are responsible for the underlying debt.

Counteroffer—A counteroffer is a statement by the offeree which has the legal effect of rejecting the offer and of proposing a new offer to the offeror.

Court—The branch of government responsible for the resolution of disputes arising under the laws of the government.

Credit—Money that a lender gives to a borrower on condition of repayment over a certain period.

Credit History—A record of an individual's debt payments.

Credit Insurance—An insurance policy that pays off credit card debt if the borrower loses his or her job, becomes disabled, or dies.

Credit Limit—The maximum amount of charges a cardholder may apply to the account.

Credit Line—The maximum amount of money available in an open-end credit arrangement such as a credit card.

Creditor—One who is owed money.

Credit Rating—A judgment of an individual consumer's ability to repay their debts, based on current and projected income and history of payment of past debts.

Credit Report—A credit report refers to the document from a credit reporting agency setting forth a credit rating and pertinent financial data concerning a person or a company, which is used in evaluating the applicant's financial stability.

Credit Reporting Agency—A company that issues credit reports on how individual consumers manage their debts and make payments.

Credit Score—A number assigned to an individual's credit rating.

Damages—In general, damages refers to monetary compensation which the law awards to one who has been injured by the actions of another, such as in the case of tortious conduct or breach of contractual obligations.

Debt—Money one person owes another.

Debt Consolidation Loan—The replacement of two or more loans with a single loan, usually with a lower monthly payment and a longer repayment period.

Debt Collector—Any person or business that regularly collects debts that are owed, or which were originally owed, to another person.

Defamation—The publication of an injurious statement about the reputation of another

Default—The condition that occurs when a consumer fails to fulfill the obligations set out in a loan.

Defendant—In a civil proceeding, the party responding to the complaint.

Defense—Opposition to the truth or validity of the plaintiff's claims.

Delinquent—Refers to a debt that has not been paid by the payment date or by the end of any grace period.

Demand for Arbitration—A unilateral filing of a claim in arbitration based on the filer's contractual or statutory right to do so.

Disclaimer—Words or conduct which tend to negate or limit warranty in the sale of goods, which in certain instances must be conspicuous and refer to the specific warranty to be excluded.

Disclosure—Disclosure is the act of disclosing or revealing that which is secret or not fully understood.

Down Payment—A partial payment of the purchase price.

Duress—Refers to the action of one person which compels another to do something he or she would not otherwise do.

Duty—The obligation, to which the law will give recognition and effect, to conform to a particular standard of conduct toward another.

Equal Credit Opportunity Act—A federal law which prohibits a creditor from discriminating against an applicant on the basis of race, religion, national origin, age, sex or marital status.

Equity—The fair market value of a home less the outstanding mortgage debt, home equity loan or line of credit, and other obligations secured by the home.

Express Warranty—A promise relating to the quality or condition of property which is usually reduced to writing.

Fair Credit Billing Act—A federal law passed by Congress in 1975 to help customers resolve billing disputes with card issuers.

Fair Credit Reporting Act—A federal law that governs what credit bureaus can report concerning an individual consumer.

Fair Debt Collection Practices Act—A federal law that governs debt collection methods.

Federal Trade Commission—The Federal Trade Commission is an agency of the federal government created in 1914 for the purpose of promoting free and fair competition in interstate commerce.

Finance Charge—The charge for using a credit card, including interest costs and other fees.

Fixed Income—Income which is unchangeable.

Forbearance—A postponement of loan payments, granted by a lender or creditor, for a temporary period of time.

Foreclosure—The procedure by which mortgaged property is sold on default of the mortgagor in satisfaction of mortgage debt.

Fraud—A false representation of a matter of fact, whether by words or by conduct, by false or misleading allegations, or by concealment of that which should have been disclosed, which deceives and is intended to deceive another, and thereby causes injury to that person.

Fraudulent Conveyance—The transfer of property for the purpose of delaying or defrauding creditors.

Free on Board (FOB)—Free on board is a commercial term that signifies a contractual agreement between a buyer and a seller to have the subject of a sale delivered to a designated place, usually either the place of shipment or the place of destination.

Garnish—To attach the wages or property of an individual.

Garnishee—A person who receives notice to hold the assets of another, which are in his or her possession, until such time as a court orders the disposition of the property.

General Damages—General damages are those damages directly referable to the breach or tortious act and which can be readily proven to have been sustained, and for which the injured party should be compensated as a matter of right.

Grace Period—The interest-free period between the transaction date and the billing date allowed by the credit card issuer provided the credit card holder does not carry a balance on their credit card.

Guarantor—One who makes a guaranty.

Guaranty—An agreement to perform in the place of another if that person reneges on a promise contained in an underlying agreement.

Home Equity Credit Line—A type of revolving credit where the borrower can borrow funds up to an established limit and the funds are secured by the borrower's home.

Homestead—The house, outbuilding, and land owned and used as a dwelling by the head of the family.

Implied Warranty—A warranty relating to the quality or condition of property that is implied by law to exist.

Impound—To place property in the custody of an official.

Improvement—The development of land or structures to increase the property value.

In Rem—Refers to actions that are against property, and concerned with the disposition of that property, rather than against the person.

Indemnification Clause—An indemnification clause in a contract refers to the agreement by one party to secure the other party against loss or damage which may occur in the future in connection with performance of the contract.

Indemnify—To hold another harmless for loss or damage which has already occurred, or which may occur in the future.

Injunction—A judicial remedy either requiring a party to perform an act, or restricting a party from continuing a particular act.

Injury—Any damage done to another's person, rights, reputation or property.

Installment Contract—An installment contract is one in which the obligation, such as the payment of money, is divided into a series of successive performances over a period of time.

Interest—An amount of money paid by a borrower to a lender for the use of the lender's money.

Interest Rate—The percentage of a sum of money charged for its use.

Introductory Rate—The low rate charged by a lender for an initial period after which the rate increases to the indexed rate or the stated interest rate.

Judge—The individual who presides over a court, and whose function it is to determine controversies.

Judgment—A judgment is a final determination by a court of law concerning the rights of the parties to a lawsuit.

Judgment Creditor—A creditor who has obtained a judgment against a debtor, which judgment may be enforced to obtain payment of the amount due.

Judgment Debtor—An individual who owes a sum of money, and against whom a judgment has been awarded for that debt.

Judgment Proof—Refers to the status of an individual who does not have the financial resources or assets necessary to satisfy a judgment.

Late Fee—A fee charged by a creditor when a payment does not post by the specified due date.

Latent Defect—A hidden defect in a product that is not ordinarily discoverable upon reasonable inspection.

Lease—A contract between two parties whereby one party transfers possession but not ownership of property to another for a specific time in return for specific consideration.

Legal Capacity—Referring to the legal capacity to sue, it is the requirement that a person bringing the lawsuit have a sound mind, be of lawful age, and be under no restraint or legal disability.

Lemon Laws—Refers to state legislation affording certain remedies to the purchasers of new or used vehicles which are discovered to have recurrent repair problems which are not able to be resolved by the manufacturer or dealer of the vehicle.

Leveraging—The process of borrowing funds at a low interest rate and investing the funds at a high rate of return.

Levy—To seize property in order to satisfy a judgment.

Liability—Liability refers to one's obligation to do or refrain from doing something, such as the payment of a debt.

Libel—The false and malicious publication, in printed form, for the purpose of defaming another.

Lien—A legal claim held by a creditor against an asset to guarantee repayment of a debt.

Liquidated Damages—An amount stipulated in a contract as a reasonable estimate of damages to be paid in the event the contract is breached.

Loan Principal—The loan principal is the amount of the debt not including interest or any other additions.

Magnuson-Moss Act—A federal law governing the placement and content of written warranties on consumer products.

Maker—As used in commercial law, the individual who executes a note.

Material Breach—A material breach refers to a substantial breach of contract which excuses further performance by the innocent party and gives rise to an action for breach of contract by the injured party.

Maturity Date—The date upon which a creditor is designated to receive payment of a debt, such as payment of the principal value of a bond to a bondholder by the issuing company or governmental entity.

Mechanic's Lien—A claim created by law for the purpose of securing a priority of payment of the price of work performed and materials furnished.

Mediation—The act of a third person in intermediating between two contending parties with a view to persuading them to adjust or settle their dispute but without the authority to make a binding decision.

Merger Clause—A merger clause is a provision in a contract which states that the written terms of the agreement may not be varied by prior or oral agreements because all such agreements are said to have merged into the writing.

Minimum Payment—The minimum amount a credit card holder can pay to keep the account from going into default.

Minor—A person who has not yet reached the age of legal competence, which is designated as 18 in most states.

Monthly Periodic Rate—The interest rate factor used to calculate the interest charges on a monthly basis, i.e., the yearly rate divided by 12.

Mortgage—A written instrument, duly executed and delivered, that creates a lien upon real estate as security for the payment of a specific debt.

Mutual Agreement—Mutual agreement refers to the meeting of the minds of the parties to a contract concerning the subject matter of the contract.

Negotiable Instrument—A signed writing which contains an unconditional promise to pay a sum of money, either on demand or at a specified time, payable to the order of the bearer.

Net Income—Gross income less deductions and exemptions proscribed by law.

Net Worth—The difference between one's assets and liabilities.

Nominal Damages—A trivial sum of money which is awarded as recognition that a legal injury was sustained, although slight.

Note—A writing which promises payment of a debt.

Novation—A novation refers to the substitution of a new party and the discharge of an original party to a contract, with the assent of all parties.

Obligee—An obligee is one who is entitled to receive a sum of money or performance from the obligor.

Obligor—An obligor is one who promises to perform or pay a sum of money under a contract.

Offeree—An offeree is the person to whom an offer is made.

Offeror—An offeror is the person who makes an offer.

Open-End Credit—Revolving credit, such as credit cards, which allow the borrower to make payments and use funds up to an established credit limit.

Option—An option is a right to purchase or lease property at an agreed upon price and terms within a specified time which is given for consideration.

Oral Agreement—An oral agreement is one which is not in writing or not signed by the parties.

Overdraft Privilege—Service offered by a bank allowing customers to borrow more than the amount on deposit in their bank account.

Overlimit Fee—A fee charged by a creditor to the consumer for a balance exceeding the consumer's credit limit.

Parol Evidence Rule—The parol evidence rule is the doctrine which holds that the written terms of an agreement may not be varied by prior or oral agreements.

Parties—The disputants.

Past Due Fee—A fee charged by a creditor to the consumer when their account is past due.

Pecuniary—A term relating to monetary matters.

Performance—Performance refers to the completion of one's contractual obligation.

Prepayment Penalty—A penalty payable by the mortgagor for early payment of the debt.

Prima Facie Case—A case which is sufficient on its face, being supported by at least the requisite minimum of evidence, and being free from palpable defects.

Principal—The amount of money owed on a loan excluding interest.

Privity of Contract—Privity of contract refers to the relationship between the parties to a contract.

Product Liability—The legal liability of manufacturers and sellers to compensate buyers, users, and even bystanders, for damages or injuries suffered because of defects in goods purchased.

Purchase Order—A purchase order is a document which authorizes a seller to deliver goods and is considered an offer which is accepted upon delivery.

Quid Pro Quo—Latin for "something for something." Refers to the exchange of promises or performances between two parties. Also refers to the legal consideration necessary to create a binding contract.

Rate of Return—The percentage gain or loss on an investment expressed as a yearly rate.

Re-Aged Account—Refers to an account status that is updated to reflect current when the account was delinquent.

Rate—Percentage a borrower pays for the use of money.

Referee's Deed—A deed given by a referee or other public officer pursuant to a court order for the sale of property.

Reformation—An equitable remedy which calls for the rewriting of a contract involving a mutual mistake or fraud.

Release—A document signed by one party, releasing claims he or she may have against another party, usually as part of a settlement agreement.

Repayment Plan—A plan devised to repay debt.

Repudiation—In contract law, refers to the declaration of one of the parties to the contract that he or she will not perform under the contract.

Rescission—The cancellation of a contract which returns the parties to the positions they were in before the contract was made.

Restatement of Contracts—The Restatement of Contracts is a series of volumes written and published by the American Law Institute (ALI) which attempts to state an orderly explanation of the current and evolving law of contracts.

Restitution—The act of making an aggrieved party whole by compensating him or her for any loss or damage sustained.

Sale—An agreement to transfer property from the seller to the buyer for a stated sum of money.

Sale and Leaseback—An agreement whereby the seller transfers property to the buyer who immediately leases the property back to the seller.

Satisfaction—The discharge and release of an obligation.

Secured Credit Card—A credit card secured by a savings deposit to ensure payment of the outstanding balance if the credit card holder defaults on payments.

Secured Loan—Borrowed money backed by collateral.

Service of Process—The delivery of legal court documents, such as a complaint, to the defendant.

Settlement—An agreement by the parties to a dispute on a resolution of the claims, usually requiring some mutual action, such as payment of money in consideration of a release of claims.

Statute of Limitations—Any law which fixes the time within which parties must take judicial action to enforce rights or thereafter be barred from enforcing them.

Stay—A judicial order suspending some action until further court order lifting the stay.

Stipulation—An admission or agreement made by parties to a lawsuit concerning the pending matter.

Strict Liability—A concept applied by the courts in product liability cases, in which a seller is liable for any and all defective or hazardous products which unduly threaten a consumer's personal safety.

Subpoena—A court issued document compelling the appearance of a witness before the court.

Subpoena Duces Tecum—A court issued document requiring a witness to produce certain document in his or her possession or control.

Substantial Performance—The performance of nearly all of the essential terms of a contract so that the purpose of the contract has been accomplished giving rise to the right to compensation.

Summons—A mandate requiring the appearance of the defendant in an action under penalty of having judgment.

Tangible Property—Property which is capable of being possessed, whether real or personal.

Trial—The judicial procedure whereby disputes are determined based on the presentation of issues of law and fact. The trier of fact, either the judge or jury, decides issues of fact and the judge decides issues of law.

Trial Court—The court of original jurisdiction over a particular matter.

Truth-In-Lending Act—A federal law which requires commercial lenders to provide applicants with detailed, accurate and understandable information relating to the cost of credit, so as to permit the borrower to make an informed decision.

Unconscionable—Refers to a bargain so one-sided as to amount to an absence of meaningful choice on the part of one of the parties, together with terms which are unreasonably favorable to the other party.

Undue Influence—The exertion of improper influence upon another for the purpose of destroying that person's free will in carrying out a particular act, such as entering into a contract.

Uniform Commercial Code (UCC)—The UCC is a code of laws governing commercial transactions which was designed to bring uniformity to the laws of the various states.

Unsecured Credit—Credit extended without collateral.

Unsecured Debt—Debt not guaranteed by the pledge of collateral, e.g. a credit card.

Unsecured Loan—An advance of money that is not secured by collateral.

Usurious Contract—A contract that imposes interest at a rate which exceeds the legally permissible rate.

Usury—An excessive rate of interest above the maximum permissible rate established by the state legislature.

Vendor—A seller.

Vitiate—To make void.

Void—Having no legal force or binding effect.

Voidable—Capable of being rendered void and unenforceable.

Voluntary Arbitration—Arbitration which occurs by mutual and free consent of the parties.

Warranty—An assurance by one party to a contract that a certain fact exists and may be relied upon by the other party to the contract.

Warranty of Fitness for a Particular Purpose—A warranty that goods purchased are suitable for the specific purpose of the buyer.

Warranty of Habitability—A warranty by a landlord that leased premises are without defects which would render the premises unusable.

Warranty of Merchantability—A warranty that goods purchased are fit for the general purpose for which they are being purchased.

BIBLIOGRAPHY AND ADDITIONAL READING

Better Business Bureau On-Line (Date Visited: May 2007) <http://www.bbbonline.org/>.

Black's Law Dictionary, Fifth Edition. St. Paul, MN: West Publishing Company, 1979.

Call For Action (Date Visited: May 2007) <http://www.callforaction.org/>.

Center for Democracy and Technology (Date Visited: May 2007) <http://www.consumerprivacyguide.org/>.

Consumer Affairs.com (Date Visited: May 2007) <http://www.consumeraffairs.com/>.

Consumer Information Center (Date Visited: May 2007) <http://www.pueblo.gsa.gov/>.

Consumer Sentinel (Date Visited: May 2007) <http://www.consumer.gov/sentinel/>.

Cornell Law School Legal Information Institute. (Date Visited: May 2007) <http://www.law.cornell.edu/>.

Direct Marketing Association (Date Visited: May 2007) <http://www.the-dma.org/>.

Equifax (Date Visited: May 2007) <http://www.equifax.com/>.

Experian (Date Visited: May 2007) <http://www.experian.com/>.

Federal Bureau of Investigation Internet Fraud Complaint Center (Date Visited: May 2007) <http://www.fbi.gov/>.

The Federal Citizen Information Center (Date Visited: May 2007) <http://www.pueblo.gsa.gov/>.

Federal Deposit Insurance Corporation (Date Visited: May 2007) <http://www.fdic.gov/>.

Federal Trade Commission (Date Visited: May 2007) <http://www.ftc.gov/>.

Identity Theft Resource Center (Date Visited: May 2007) <http://www.idtheftcenter.org/>.

Internal Revenue Service (Date Visited: May 2007) <http://www.irs.gov/>.

The International Association of Lemon Law Administrators (IALLA) (Date Visited: May 2007) <http://www.ialla.net/>.

National Conference of Commissioners on Uniform State Laws - Official Site. (Date Visited: May 2007) <http://www.nccusl.org/>.

National Consumer's League (Date Visited: May 2007) <http://natlconsumersleague.org/>.

National Highway and Traffic Safety Administration (Date Visited: May 2007) <http://www.nhtsa.dot.gov/>.

National Institute of Standards and Technology (Date Visited: May 2007) <http://www.nist.gov/>.

National Safety Council (Date Visited: May 2007) <http://www.nsc.org/>.

Nolo On-Line Encyclopedia (Date Visited: May 2007) <http://www.nolo.com/>.

Online Public Education Network (Date Visited: May 2007) <http://www.internetalliance.org/>.

Privacy Rights Clearinghouse (Date Visited: May 2007) <http://www.privacyrights.org/>.

TransUnion (Date Visited: May 2007) <http://www.transunion.com/>.

Truste (Date Visited: May 2007) <http://www.truste.org/>.

United States Consumer Product Safety Commission (Date Visited: May 2007) <http://www.cpsc.gov/>.

United States Department of Justice (Date Visited: May 2007) <http://www.usdoj.gov/>.

United States General Accounting Office (Date Visited: May 2007) <http://www.gao.gov/>.

United States Office of the Attorney General (Date Visited: May 2007) <http://www.usdoj.gov/ag/>.